Capital Campaign Playbook

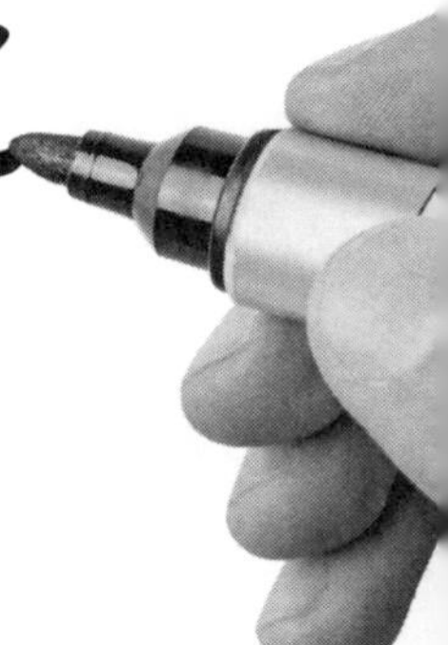

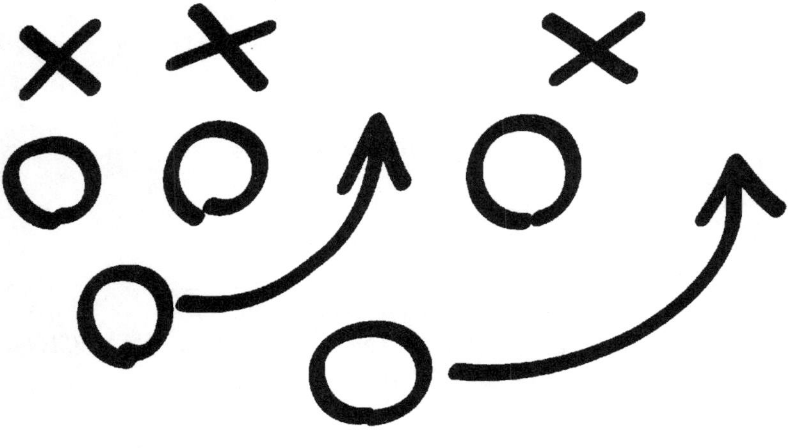

Capital Campaign Playbook

A Church Consultant's Gameplan

GREG GIBBS

Foreword by Will Mancini

B&H PUBLISHING
NASHVILLE, TENNESSEE

978-1-5359-9569-6

Published by B&H Publishing Group
Nashville, Tennessee

Dewey Decimal Classification: 332
Subject Heading: FUNDRAISING / CHURCH FINANCE / FINANCE

Cover design by Mark Karis. Photos © oneclearvision/istock and Sasun Bughdaryan/shutterstock. Author photo by Chris Cook.

1 2 3 4 5 6 7 • 24 23 22 21 20

For Rocky Miskelly, who believed in
God's redeeming plan for me.

For Mom and Dad, Lew and Sheron Gibbs, who taught
me to love the church and serve it out of gratitude.

For Andrea, who has been my inspiration
for virtually everything that matters.

"But me—who am I, and who are these my people, that we should presume to be giving something to you? Everything comes from you; all we're doing is giving back what we've been given from your generous hand. As far as you're concerned, we're homeless, shiftless wanderers like our ancestors, our lives mere shadows, hardly anything to us. GOD, *our God, all these materials—these piles of stuff for building a house of worship for you, honoring your Holy Name—it all came from you! It was all yours in the first place!"*

1 Chronicles 29:14–16 (MSG)

Welcome!

This guide is intended to help leadership teams at churches who are considering a capital campaign. My aim is to encourage those new to capital campaigns and experienced leaders as well. I am optimistic that you can design a campaign to be life-giving and powerful! This playbook outlines critical questions to ask and allows for a "workspace" to jot notes and get ready for the exciting times ahead!

This is called a playbook because it contains much of what consultants use to help church leaders through a capital campaign. Combined, my colleagues and I have helped conduct hundreds of campaigns over the years. I have assembled a time-tested series of elements and features that have been successfully used in these campaigns for decades. This is a ship's log of our collective journey with churches across the theological and geographic landscape.

As a twenty-year consultant who earns a living coaching church leaders, many might ask if I am running the risk of losing opportunities to consult by disclosing my trade secrets in this manual. Perhaps I am. But I believe as leaders use this manual as a diagnostic tool, they will recognize the difference between simple and easy.

While church capital campaigns can seem rather boilerplate on the surface, the particulars of each campaign can vary widely. This playbook is meant to provide discussion starters, not discussion "enders," by getting all of the basic stuff on the table right away. It is written as a robust insider's guide but will not replace the value of a strategic outsider.

What I have written on these pages is a culmination of listening to and learning from friends from hundreds of churches, colleagues from Cargill Associates and Kensington Church, and mostly in collaboration with some of the finest consultants I have known—the team at Auxano.

May God bless you and your church!

Greg Gibbs
Lead Navigator, Auxano

Contents

Foreword

While there are many kinds of experts, most fit into one of two categories. The first kind of expert is the smart person that you don't really enjoy being around. Their fine-tuned knowledge, however valuable, is overshadowed by either the impersonal way they deliver their intelligence or by their lack of passion for the subject. The second kind of expert is the person who loves to serve with their insight. These kinds of people are joyful, generous, and life-giving. They transcend the transactional to become trustworthy guides who are delightful to follow.

Greg Gibbs is a wonderful model of the latter kind of expert.

As the leader of Auxano's generosity and capital campaign team, Greg is one of the finest consultants I've had the privilege to know. He loves Jesus and serves the church as the bride of Christ. His heart for God is paired with a razor-sharp mind and super-savvy people skills.

With the book you now hold, Greg has done something unprecedented. Ever since the late 1960s, consultants have preyed on the local church's lack of specialized knowledge in the areas of fundraising. At no time has one of these consultants dared to deliver the essence of their expertise in written form. Of course books have been penned, but not like this one. This book is a carefully curated treasure chest. Each chapter contains twenty-four-karat wisdom and solid gold nuggets to fill your leadership pockets. Greg has been panning for a long time, sifting through all of the silt and dirt and grit in stream after stream for three decades.

The call to lead God's people is not for the faint of heart. There will always be challenges. But when it comes to increasing the generosity of your people, you don't need to be left wondering or wandering. Take hold of the principles and practices from a trustworthy guide. Enjoy the journey. Use this book to lead God's people into a life of generosity that is one of the greatest secrets of our Godlikeness. Use this book to rally people to God's dreams that unleash the kingdom on Earth as it is in heaven.

Will Mancini

Introduction

I can make this introduction short by revealing my attitude right up front:

I love capital campaigns.

About twenty years ago, my friend Rev. Rocky Miskelly introduced me to the world of Church Capital Campaigns. Not only had I never been through one, but I found myself unsteady at the helm—a young, recently promoted senior pastor of a ten-year-old church plant building its first building ever.

Rocky was consulting with Cargill Associates, one of the long-standing firms in our country formed in 1976. I would eventually learn about Dr. Robert Cargill and his family and the many churches and universities that the family and company have helped throughout the decades. I would gain a profound respect for them. I remember hearing some dramatic tale (like only Southerners can tell) of how RSI and Cargill started about the same time back in the wonder years. I have forgotten the details and that is not important. But my testimony about this work emanates out of the amazing experience our church in Kalamazoo, Michigan, had as a result of Rocky's work with us.

If you ever hear me talk about it in person, it goes something like this:

> *I knew we needed to raise money for the church, and I had heard that consultants were necessary to accomplish this. In my naivety (and arrogance) as a very young pastor, I thought,* ***"Let's let this guy come in and do what he must, so I can get back to the real work of ministry."*** *But during the course of the months he was with us, our congregation grew spiritually in unexpected ways. At least they were unexpected to me. People's faith in God grew. Married couples had unprecedented conversations about their lives and the purpose of their resources. Andrea and I made a commitment to the church that was way beyond our own ability to fulfill. And you could have probably guessed that God, through extraordinary circumstances, enabled us to fulfill that pledge. We learned that the most emotional, vulnerable, underdeveloped part of most of many people's walk as a disciple of Jesus was in regard to their money (well, God's money). And when we studied how much Jesus was obsessed with talking about it, we realized that doing a good campaign around generosity and "above-and-beyond" giving was the real work of ministry.*

Through a series of circumstances, I later joined the Cargill team full-time and Rocky took me under his wing. Before I knew it, I was consulting on a dozen campaigns each year. Eventually I joined the staff of Kensington Church, my home church just outside of Detroit, where I, along with a team, led two separate campaigns targeting $25M each for buildings, church planting, and global missions through Kensington.

During the economic downturn of 2008–2010, Detroit was ground zero for economic stress. It was in that context that my friend Alex Calder and I learned some difficult lessons about how to pastor people through the hard times when it came to the application of faith to financial resources.

I joined the team at Auxano after conducting more than one hundred campaigns while continuing on staff at Kensington for the next ten years. Auxano, a consulting firm founded by author and consulting genius Will Mancini, is a kind of SEAL team of church coaches. In their early days, the team was primarily two guys—Will Mancini and Jim Randall—who worked to perfect the process of helping churches discover organizational clarity.

The genesis of this consulting platform began in Will's creative mind and was eventually chronicled in his book *Church Unique* (published in 2008). As an organization, Auxano deploys consultants called "Navigators" across the country. They work with churches of all shapes and sizes in applying Mancini's insistence on "stunning clarity" to the process of discipleship in mission-minded churches.

The Resourcing Division of Auxano takes the engine of clarity (our company DNA) and applies it to capital fundraising and generosity development for churches. The following chapters are the tools and techniques that I have learned over the years and now practice with my colleagues at Auxano.

I believe that this is a fairly comprehensive manual. The church capital campaign industry has been perfecting a set of practices over the decades with only slight variations in style and substance from one consulting company to the next. I say this with great respect as I personally know many of the stellar men and women who do this work.

I am intending to give the trade secrets away because I believe doing so will help churches get a head start on the creation and execution of a successful capital campaign. And like many other pastors and consultants that I have come to know, this is the way we are serving God on this earth—helping His church be the best it can be by sharing the tools we have developed and refined over the years.

The following areas of importance are each framed in a "set of three"—three questions or three ideas or three concepts. It is meant to be a quick reference guide. Please use these for discussion and deliberation. Time spent with this playbook will help get your team ready for raising capital or "over-and-above" giving.

I firmly believe that great consultants, coaches, and navigators are still needed in the church in America. Perhaps more than ever before. But if the contents of this book accelerate knowledge and expertise in this area—the capital funding of the dreams of the church—then I will be satisfied. All of the flights, rental cars, and airport meals will have been worth it.

Oh, and thanks, Rocky, for believing that God could use me for His church when I wasn't totally convinced of that. Everyone needs a Rocky.

Chapter One

Three Waves of Process

When people in the church mention a capital campaign, they are almost always thinking about one phase of it—the public phase. People remember or focus on that part because it is the part where church leaders are talking, preaching, praying, meeting, and conversing about the projects with the whole congregation. But there are actually multiple waves and a lot of work before we ever go public with asking for over-and-above financial contributions.

In the pre-campaign waves, we are establishing our readiness as a church to enter a campaign. There is a good chance that if you are reading this, you are in that phase. At a very basic level, the inquiry starts with "How much does our project cost, and will our people give that much?"

Beyond the basic question is the idea that the preparation phase is as important (or more important) than the public phase. From due diligence to establishing appropriate targets to assessing congregational buy-in, this phase is where the greatest victories and mishaps may actually occur.

Then, we realize there is still another level. For churches that want to conduct a discipleship-based campaign, we discover an extraordinary opportunity. The campaign can be a massive greenhouse for growing people's commitment to Christ and their understanding of a life that is "true life" (1 Tim. 6:17–19).

This is why, in part, this book has been assembled. Because when there is thoughtfulness in regard to shaping the campaign, it can be an amazing experience filled with celebration and excitement instead of a dull but necessary endeavor dreaded by church leaders. The challenge is to aim for a best-case scenario: that faith in God and commitment to the church grow in a special and intense way.

To meet this challenge, church leaders should pay attention to the process in three waves:

Discover
Design
Disciple

Discover

I have the privilege and honor of coaching the senior leadership of churches under the umbrella of Auxano, a company that is the category-leader in regard to Vision Clarity. The coaches (called Auxano Navigators) don't know where else to start but with questions about clarity. Being clear is uber-critical in any organization—especially in the church.

And if things have been fuzzy for a while about a church, its mission, its effectiveness, its future, its focus, or anything else, a capital campaign will expose that lack of clarity. There is nothing that exposes our organizational soft spots like a campaign.

Members of the church will put up with being a bit in the dark regarding church leadership and their intentions most of the time.

We love our church and for good reasons. But when church leaders start to say things like, "Let's pray about giving the largest gift we've ever given" or "Please consider supporting the church with a financial gift beyond your current support," all of a sudden people care deeply about clarity.

They are asking themselves, "Why would I give even more to my church? What is so important that I should be praying audacious prayers about my increased giving? I'm not even sure I understand what's going on anyway."

The discovery process in a campaign starts with clarity. It requires uncovering (or being honest about) how much clarity exists in our congregation. Do people know the answers to the five irreducible questions of clarity: What? Why? How? When? and Where? In other words, before we start measuring for curtains in the new fellowship hall, we need to find out if people know where we are headed. Some churches need a bit of a clarity "time-out."

Five Irreducible Questions of Leadership

Frame Component	Icon	Irreducible Question of Leadership	Missional Reorientation
Mission		What are we doing?	^{m}*Mandate*
Values		Why are we doing it?	^{m}*Motives*
Strategy		How are we doing it?	^{m}*Map*
Measures		When are we successful?	^{m}*Marks*
Vision Proper		Where is God taking us?	^{m}*Mountaintop + Milestones*

Figure 1.1

NOTE: For more help with this, read Will Mancini's landmark work *Church Unique*, which outlines how churches can articulate their identity and direction with stunning clarity.

Before moving forward with a capital campaign, church leaders may need a time of refining and honing their vision and mission. Then they may need to clarify and communicate this to the congregation. Then, and only then, will the congregation be ready to hear about projects that support that clear idea of a God-inspired future together.

I recently worked with a church in Oklahoma who originally hired me to help them conduct a capital campaign. As we started to ask the Five Irreducible Questions, it became evident that capital improvements were the least of their concerns. With a senior pastor in succession, an aging congregation, a struggling second campus, and no clear understanding of the next steps for their organizational health, there was more murkiness than would allow for an effective campaign. We took a needed time-out from campaign talk and began to chip away at their real need for organizational clarity and a focused plan for the future of their ministry.

Another important aspect that is critical to understand is that many of our churches are still made up of people from several generations, including the Builder generation, of whom many are financially supportive of the church. Barna and other researchers have revealed the differences in generational views of "building buildings" as well as giving behavior in general. The over-representation of the Builder generation in the positions of leadership and influence often leads the church to equate progress with building construction.

At the same time, so many churches are wondering why they aren't connecting with the younger generations, Generation X and Millennial leaders. There are books written about this (this is not one of them), and this is an important pursuit when it comes to understanding the best direction for the church. Knowing the language and perspective of the generations in your church is critical. Some readers may need to put this book down and not consider pursuing a capital campaign until there is a better understanding of these dynamics and how they will play out at their church.

Church leaders should have solid and clear responses to questions like:

> *What is our vision for the future?*
>
> *Who are we and who are we becoming through God's help?*
>
> *How will the projects being considered in this campaign help get us to that destination?*

When we have a sense of how much vision "equity" we have with the people, we will know better how to communicate the importance of the capital projects in light of that.

Reality Check

The other part of the discovery process is assessing our reality. It is a look at our current data—the indicators of congregational engagement, involvement, and financial support.

Why? *Because the greatest predictor of future behavior is past behavior.* We operate in faith and optimism, but we also have an eye on the numbers and ground ourselves in reality. It is recommended that church leaders assess both *Capacity* and *Inclination.*

Looking at capacity answers the most popular question a consultant hears when it comes to campaigns: *How much can our church raise?* And the idea of inclination delves into the more difficult question to answer: *What will our congregation actually give?*

Capacity

In the capital campaign world, the church's general budget revenue is used as a top-level predictive tool regarding the church's capacity. In other words, if we are simply making an educated guess or general estimate, we start with the church's annual operating revenue and then multiply that by some factor: 1 times that number, or 1.5 times, 2 times, or 3 times.

Prior to the downturn of 2008–2010, the church capital campaign world was somewhat straightforward and fairly predictable:

Church Operating Budget = X
Capital Gifts Over Three Years = 2 or 3 times X

When I was trained almost twenty years ago, the major capital campaign consulting companies for churches in America were groups like RSI, Cargill (for whom I worked in the early 2000s), Injoy, and a few others. And with rare exceptions, these companies would regularly lead churches to campaigns that resulted in double or triple the annual income in capital gifts over a three-year period.

Things have changed—the dynamics in play before 2008 are very different than those today. The two most common stats are no longer the norm. Back in the day, most campaigns garnered at least two times general income and most campaigns were over a three-year collection period. It was clockwork. Like the Chicago Cubs never getting to the World Series. Well, that was then and this is now. These dynamics have shifted considerably. And just look at those Cubs!

Current Trend

Churches are bold if they estimate that multi-year pledges will amount to anything larger than 1.5 times the church's income.

Inclination

Perhaps even more important than a congregation's capacity to give is their collective inclination to do so. What this means is that a person or congregation may have a capacity to give X, but there is another factor in play: What are they likely to give to the project at hand? Not what could they give but what are they *likely to give*?

Some projects tend to motivate people to give to their full capacity. Some may even cause people to stretch beyond what is comfortable as an act of faith.

Others, not so much.

Much of this is connected with the emotional tie-in and buy-in associated with varying aspects of church life. A part of it is connected with something tangible that we "get to see" when the money has been invested. This is why *Debt* or *Dirt* campaigns are the hardest to explain and connect with vision as well as people's hearts. When we are retiring a mortgage or securing land, these are very important strategies for church life, but are just more difficult to create emotional support for. And this is why *New Church Building* or *Sanctuary Renovation* can garner lots of passion. It affects everybody in significant ways and is tied into our spiritual practices and places.

Continuum of Likely Results Based on Campaign Focus

.5 1.0 1.5 2.0 2.5 3.0 3.5

Debt Land Renovation Addition New Location

Notes:

Figure 1.2

Where would you rank your individual components or projects on a 1 to 10 scale, with 1 being "very difficult to gain emotional buy-in" and 10 being "easy to gain buy-in, people will be ecstatic"?

Project Buy-in Assessment										
	LOW BUY-IN									HIGH BUY-IN
	1	2	3	4	5	6	7	8	9	10
Project 1										
Project 2										
Project 3										
Project 4										

Figure 1.3

My friend Rocky Miskelly is a passionate, lifelong football fan of the University of Mississippi. He would explain the importance of understanding congregational buy-in by using football fans as an analogy as he talked about Ole Miss.

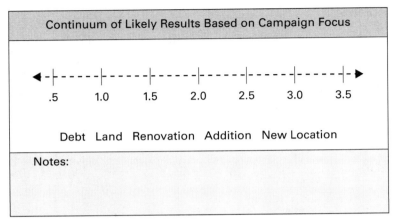

He describes the difference between a "fan" and a "supporter" of the football team. A fan likes to cheer for the team, and a supporter writes a check to fund the team. Just like a great college football program, you need both fans and supporters in the church. But it would be helpful to know who is in what classification before a major project is underway.

Unfortunately, we have a hard time in church capital campaigns figuring out whether people will be fans of a capital project or supporters. And if they are supporters, to what degree will they be supportive? What is their sense of buy-in? Can we identify the biggest challenges we will face when asking people to fund this particular initiative?

Jot down some of those challenges here:

NOTE: The top-notch consulting firms will have a formal assessment tool that allows for a "test" of the congregation's level of support during the planning phase so that church leaders don't get surprised during the public phase (when it is often too late to make adjustments).

The group at Aly Sterling Philanthropy offers the benefits of a formal study:

- Do I have a large enough donor base to support my goal?
- Does the project make sense and offer a concrete solution?
- Do I have the support of leadership?
- How much should we expect to raise?

- Is now the right time to host a capital campaign?
- What questions do potential donors have about the project?
- Who are potential major gift prospects/campaign leaders?

Capacity versus Project Cost

I continue to be befuddled by churches that create wish lists and dream projects and spend time and money designing something they have no business designing. Not because churches shouldn't dream or be creative, but because without some grounding in financial reality, it can burn up energy unnecessarily.

Some churches really slow down progress by having to retreat from plans because they are way beyond the scope of what can be raised. Should we not have some sense of what our church is likely to give (and whether or not we are willing to borrow the rest) before we start designing with no financial parameters? If I were shopping for a house, a car, or budgeting for renovation in my personal life, I would start with the answer to the question, "How much can I afford to spend?" or "Am I willing to borrow money to renovate my kitchen?" Churches seem to get this in reverse order. I have met with more than a few churches that have an estimated cost for their project that is four or five times their annual budget or more.

When I discover this, I hope and pray that the leadership has not been casting vision or creating excitement about a project that they will not be able to afford. If they have been talking it up, we are immediately thrown into a back-peddling exercise before we can start a fund-raising campaign. Or the church will put itself into a position of borrowing more than they ever imagined. This undesirable outcome is the clear result of not gathering all of the necessary information to lead well.

The 4 Advisors: Architect, Builder, Banker, and Fundraising Expert

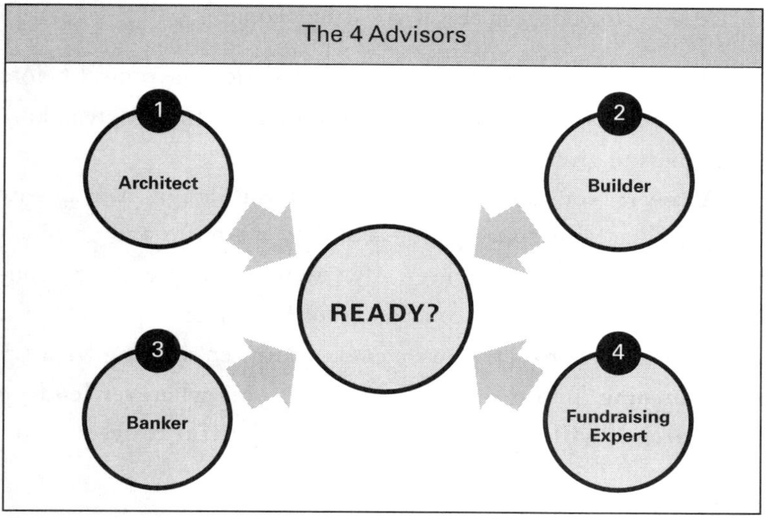

Figure 1.4

Understanding readiness is like a four-legged table. Without each of these professional advisors weighing in, there may be a missing and critical component of leading the church well.

- **Architects can answer,** "How will we design something to meet our needs primarily and our wants secondarily?"
- **Builders can answer,** "When can we start, how long will it take, and what will it likely cost?"
- **Bankers can answer,** "What will a financial institution lend us for this project should we choose to borrow either short- or long-term?"

- **Fundraising experts can answer,** "How much will the congregation likely give to a project like this, and what is the best approach to engaging and motivating people?"

People often ask: "Don't you have to design the project before you know the cost and whether or not it matches the congregation's willingness to give?"

Answer: Not really. No matter what you design, it is against the odds that your congregation will defy the norm and go much beyond three times giving even if we were in the pre–2008 economy. So that becomes the top border (or highest level possible) if it were a cash-only project. As we mentioned earlier, **starting with 1.5 times income** (in a three-year campaign) **plus whatever lending the church is willing to service is a more fruitful conversation**.

Questions to Consider

Do we have the most helpful and necessary information and feedback from the four advisors mentioned above? What do we know so far?

The 4 Advisors Assessment	
____ Architect	
____ Builder	
____ Banker	
____ Fundraising Expert	

Figure 1.5

Are we willing to borrow money for our projects? Have we considered the gap between our project cost and our likely giving amount?

(Estimate the project cost and subtract the likely giving amount from that below.)

Project Cost Equation		
Project Cost		________________
Likely Capital Receipts	–	________________
Difference via Mortgage	=	________________

Figure 1.6

Have we estimated the cash flow projection and how that may impact borrowing, start and end times, and more? In other words, when the congregation pledges X, it comes in over time—sometimes two or three years—and not in a lump sum.

Another frequently asked question is, "How much of the pledged amount can we expect to be fulfilled?" This is another statistic that doesn't seem to be going in the right direction. When I first started coaching campaigns two decades ago, we would regularly see 90–95 percent of pledges fulfilled. Much of the industry talk these days is much more conservative, and churches are encouraged to budget for 80–85 percent of total pledges unless a robust follow-up process is executed.

Chapter 17 highlights the effort that can be made in the post-pledge era of the campaign as a follow-up or follow-through on campaign promises and pledges. One way or the other, it is recommended that a cash flow projection be made to help with financial strategy and project completion time lines.

3-Year Campaign Estimates (conservative)		
Year 1 Capital Giving	Year 2 Capital Giving	Year 3 Capital Giving
$ ____________	$ ____________	$ ____________
(30% of pledged)	(29% of pledged)	(28% of pledged)

Figure 1.7

2-Year Campaign Estimates (conservative)	
Year 1 Capital Giving	Year 2 Capital Giving
$ ____________	$ ____________
(45% of pledged)	(40% of pledged)

Figure 1.8

Planning Tool

Have we taken into consideration the impact the years of capital campaign giving may have on the general budget? Are we willing to plan to slow our expectations of year over year increase and budget conservatively?

Design

The due diligence required in the Discover phase is crucial. Once that information is compiled, we are ready to begin designing the campaign.

Some people bristle at the word *campaign*, connecting it with the seamy side of political elections. But the word simply means to "work in an organized and active way toward a goal." And the church is an institution with so many worthy goals! So, what is the "organized way" we work toward achieving our goal?

Timing of the Campaign

It isn't a difficult decision, but it does require some thought. We need to decide whether the public phase of the campaign will happen between Labor Day and Christmas or between New Year's Day and Easter. It is almost that simple.

The following diagram models the two quarters ahead of the public phase necessary to do a best practice campaign. Time is needed for ramp-up, planning, and training.

The following diagram uses the Discover, Design, Disciple waves, and shows the two most often utilized times of the church calendar for the public phase:

Church Calendar for the Public Phase		
Labor Day – Christmas	OR	**New Year's – Easter**
DISCOVER	DESIGN	DISCIPLE
(Readiness)	(Silent Phase)	(Public Phase)
Q2 ----------→	**Q3** ----------→	**Q4**
	OR	
Q3 ----------→	**Q4** ----------→	**Q1**

Figure 1.9

Since the campaign needs to capture the attention and focus of the entire church, the question is: *When can we clear the calendar to focus on the campaign?*

Summer is almost never a good time. I say "almost" because of the rare exception of one client church I coached whose attendance increased during the summer (it was a resort town). But for most churches, summer time is more like a ghost town.

Length of the Collection Period

As was mentioned earlier, back in the day this really wasn't a discussion. If there was any debate at all it was about the difference between a three-year collection period and a five-year period. Many non-church entities (universities, nonprofits, etc.) would do a five-year pledge period.

These days, the options seem to be one, two, or three years.

Three-year campaigns are still in the majority but are quickly being outrun by two-year campaigns as the ever-increasing collection period of choice. The reason many churches are decreasing their pledge collection period is mostly speculative and anecdotal. However, the data points to drive the research are building steadily.

I met with a church staff in San Jose, California, a year ago, and as a man in my late forties it became quickly evident that I was the oldest guy in the room by far. I met their young CFO at a Pushpay event I was speaking at in Redmond, Washington, and he invited me to come visit with them about capital campaign consultancy.

They explained their upcoming gala was an event that they were planning to receive gifts and pledges (mostly gifts). In that Northern California context, it was a black-tie dinner and vision presentation, and people would be expected to bring checks and commitments. It was basically a one-year run-up to a one-day campaign. I was a fish out of water. Like an old dog befuddled by new tricks, I have since had to unseat my bias toward the three-year campaign plan I was trained to coach.

The more I meet young leaders in young congregations, this seems to be the tendency. There is so much transience in the congregation—young people moving around, building careers, "moving on," etc.—that talking about three years from now seems like an eternity.

Ben Stroup gives some thoughtful consideration to this topic when he writes, "The challenge of every campaign is getting enough people to buy-in, commit, give, and fulfill on their initial financial pledge throughout the entire effort to ensure initial goals are met. As churches struggle to find a new tempo in the dance with the donor, the short-term capital campaign approach seems to be a viable option for those looking to make an immediate impact and clearly communicate the ministry value of every dollar raised."[1]

Stroup cites 5 reasons to consider a shorter time period:

1. The *insecurity* that seems to drive people financially these days makes three years feel like a very *long time* (especially younger people).
2. It is difficult to maintain people's *focus* with competition from other nonprofits over a long period of time.
3. The *proximity* of time the church plans to use the funds is important (how quickly are they needed?).
4. Churches need to demonstrate a *return* on investment sooner rather than later (it is hard to keep giving consistently when people see or experience no fruit from their generosity)
5. The *effectiveness* of an eighteen-month to two-year collection period is almost the same

> in total dollars as the traditional three-year period (though this is still a small sample group overall).[2]

Dr. Clint Grider, one of Auxano's principals and a philanthropic expert, reminds us that a discipleship-based campaign framework can allow for a very different kind of process that may take longer:

> A relational process will lead people to grow in their focus, confidence, and generosity during the collection period and beyond. Sometimes church leaders don't understand the critical importance of deeper, more purposeful engagement of givers after commitments are made. In some cases, this may make a longer commitment period more effective in cultivating discipleship.[3]

A popular format right now is the One Fund, which offers churches an alternative to the traditional capital campaign. It is meant to develop generosity in all givers as they increase their giving and is collected into one fund (thus the name) instead of into multiple funds (general, capital, missions, etc.). The idea is that the church leadership can parcel off or budget the necessary funds to do capital projects—particularly ones that aren't as directly vision-based (think "roof repair").

There are mixed reviews in the early years of the One Fund approach. Some appreciate the simplicity and directness of not having multiple asks for the congregation. The One Fund helps focus churches toward the regular nurturing of people toward a life of generosity instead of the high emphasis only during a special campaign.

Other leaders have reported that, in reality, the approach is merely a semantic difference to what churches have aimed to do for years. In essence, it becomes a series of one-year generosity campaigns, no matter what we call it. In the end, it can look quite similar to what many mainline churches have done for a long time via their annual stewardship campaigns. This is because early experiences of a few hundred churches have shown that this methodology ultimately requires a kind of special "campaigning" every year anyway. In essence, it is a good way to shepherd generosity but should not be advertised as "never having to run a campaign again."

NOTE OF ADVICE: For multi-year campaigns, it is important to pay attention to two factors that likely increase giving. One is how many Decembers fall in the collection window, because December is a big giving month. Another is how many calendar years are touched by the collection window. You can have an eighteen-month to two-year campaign that traverses three tax years depending on when it starts and ends. This is a great advantage to contributors who are tax aware and tax deduction savvy. (Of course, charitable contribution deductions in the United States are constantly being threatened, so who knows what condition they are in by the time you are reading this paragraph.)

For another perspective on this, consider thoughts from Chuck Klein on this discussion about length of campaign:[4]

1. New people. As we have become a more transient society, it is probable that many of your consistent attendees—and financial contributors—were not with you three years ago. Study your records; how much turnover in membership and attendance have you experienced in that time frame? More telltale, how many of your new members can articulate vision that you presented over two years ago?

2. Unsettled economy. Today's economic climate can make it difficult for people to see short-term, much less commit long-term. Such uncertainty results in people giving conservatively. Others are unable to give now but often will when approached at a later—but sooner!—time under different personal circumstances. An extra twelve months unnecessarily delays their support and participation.

3. Generational perspectives. Today's young adults hesitate to make a three-year pledge, yet will give to causes they deem just and admirable. This is particularly true of projects that are well-planned and clearly articulated. Similarly, seniors on a fixed income can be reluctant to fill out a commitment card, viewing it more as a promissory note than promise to fulfill. Many will give to a short-term or make a one-time large gift but never fill out a pledge card.

4. Campaign fatigue. Leaders wary of "burning out" their people would do well to shorten the program. Some church leaders choose a three-year term to keep a longer period between campaigns, but this adversely impacts the momentum for many givers. Back-to-back one-year campaigns can cause even quicker burnout.

Such an approach carries less intensity with each passing year, and we've never seen successive one-year programs yield the fruit of singular, longer campaigns.

Brian Kluth, senior pastor and long-time generosity consultant, reminds us that one-year campaigns can be appropriate if the size of the capital need is less than half of the church's annual budget.

Questions to Consider

Have we discussed both the time of year we are inclined to hold the public phase of the campaign? What month and year are we anticipating the collection of pledges? (___/___)

Does our church (particularly staff) have the appetite to "clear the calendar" so that the capital campaign can be emphasized? In what ministry area will we struggle most to suspend our normal flow of activity?

List the biggest challenges to focusing on the campaign based on the time of year we anticipate conducting the public phase:

1. ______________________________

2. ______________________________

3. ______________________________

Have we considered the pros and cons of shorter rather than longer campaigns?

Take some time for a quick evaluation of each:

Risk – Benefit		
	RISK	BENEFIT
1-Year		
2-Year		
3-Year		

Figure 1.10

Shaping the Narrative

Making the "Case for Support" is an essential part of campaign design. This is the story to be told about what is happening at the church that is compelling us to ask for additional financial support from its members. We are "making the case." This represents what the business world would call a proposal or academia would call a white paper.

Key Principle: Until we have agreement at the top level of leadership about our Case for Support, we cannot start communicating widely or it will breed confusion or backpedaling.

The common phrase "singing from the same song sheet" applies here for sure. Best practice campaigns have a clear case and ask leadership to "sing" from it so that the people of the church aren't hearing different things depending on whom they ask.

One of the most helpful Auxano tools for achieving clarity through our case for support narrative is a repurposing of Mancini's Five Irreducible Questions. It becomes an outline to help in the initial draft. The questions are listed here in a reshaped manner for brainstorming the church's Case for Support:

What? What are we doing or what project or projects demand us to ask for additional funding? Describe the project, its cost (or estimated cost), and "show" if a rendering, plan, or picture could help with clarity.

NOTES and IDEAS:

Why? Why are we pursuing this and why now? Are there connections with our long-term vision as a church that drive us to consider this campaign? Is there a goal or deeply held value that would cause the urgency around this campaign?

NOTES and IDEAS:

How? How do we propose to accomplish this in terms of campaign timing and how will we engage our people? Describe the plan for engaging people and the collection period process and length.

NOTES and IDEAS:

When? When do we know we have been successful both financially and in other ways? Is there an element of discipleship that will take people to a new level of engagement with God and His church? How does increased generosity represent a spiritual success (in terms of devotion to God) beyond meeting the funding need?

NOTES and IDEAS:

Where? As we look to the future, is this campaign representing where God seems to be taking us? Is there a trajectory that follows an if/then statement like "If we are able to complete this, then we can see God using it to bring about _____ ?" Describe the desired future of the church that we can see with eyes of faith. What dream does this fulfill?

NOTES and IDEAS:

Communicating through Concentric Circles

Whether we call this Concentric Circles of Communication or Cascading Communication, the idea here is that the most effective way to breed ownership of any idea is a strategic "rollout." This requires describing the organization of the church in categories from the inside-out or the top-down and then following this as a pattern of seeking feedback and ownership.

For example, an organization outside the church may use an organization chart. The president would communicate first to vice-presidents, and then to managers, then assistant managers and then to employees. The key to this is that each "level" has the opportunity to ask questions and weigh in, both increasing ownership and refining the messaging itself.

In the case of churches, many have either an official or unofficial sense of rings of involvement. Rick Warren of Saddleback Church popularized the Core, Committed, Congregation, Crowd, and Community to describe this:

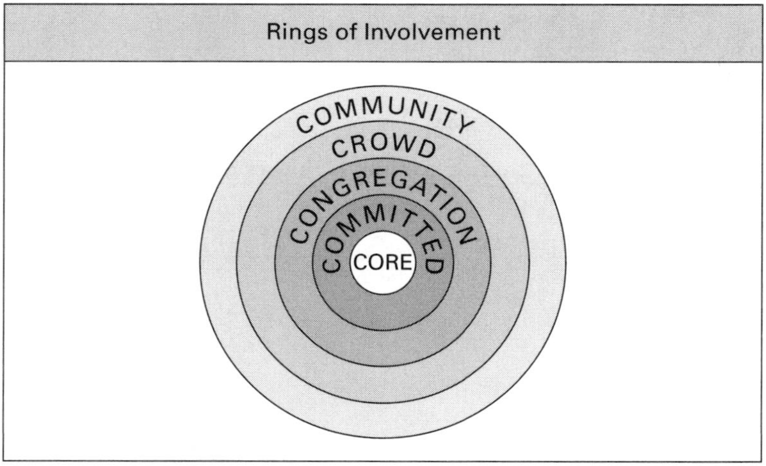

Figure 1.11

But every church likely has a pretty solid understanding of these layers or "rings" in their context.

Here are a few examples:

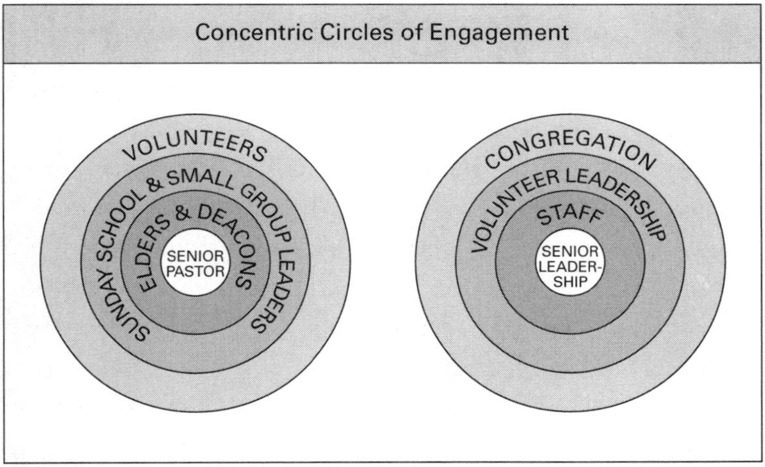

Figure 1.12

What are your layers or concentric circles of engagement?

List them here with the regularity or pace of their meeting rhythm:

Group Meeting (weekly, monthly, other?)

1. ______________________________

2. ______________________________

3. ______________________________

4. ______________________________

5. ______________________________

6. ______________________________

Use this graphic (or create your own) to sketch out a series of concentric circles that represent the rollout of the campaign idea at your church.

Concentric Circles of Engagement Worksheet

What are your layers of "concentric circles" of engagement?

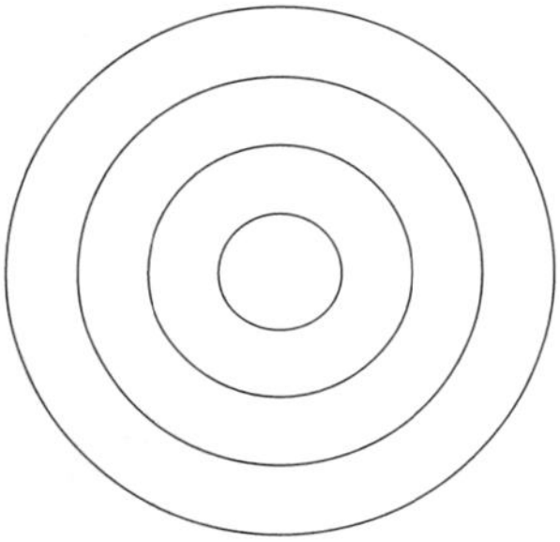

Figure 1.13

More Questions to Consider

Do we have a regular pattern of meeting with or communicating with the people in the "rings" of our communication circle?

Whether through email, newsletter, weekend messages, in person, groups, or classes, etc.—how can we best communicate the importance of our projects to people who need to hear about them and give feedback?

What are the best venues and gatherings to communicate and gather feedback?

List those venues here: (for example, Sunday morning, leader meetings, staff meetings, etc.)

1. ______________________________

2. ______________________________

3. ______________________________

4. ______________________________

5. ______________________________

Disciple

This is the best-kept secret of capital campaigns: **People can go to a new level in their devotion to Christ and His church.** People can also grow in their understanding of generosity, dependence on God, and meaningful living.

Church leaders can capitalize on this opportunity to play a bit of "catch-up" in the category of teaching about a generous life. We rarely come across a church that feels like they are ahead of the game when it comes to the connection between faith and money. Quite frankly, a majority of pastors tend to avoid the topic unless absolutely necessary, making giving less of a spiritual practice as a result.

> If you catch a member of the congregation in a moment of candor, they will often reveal in hushed tones, "The only time our pastor talks about money is when we are behind budget."

I admit I was one of those pastors back in the day. Can you really blame us? Money is rarely talked about in seminary, and people have so much dysfunction and emotion around the topic, the "risk vs. reward" of broaching the subject does not seem to go in our favor. Most of us see the topic of giving in teaching as the eating-your-vegetables part of pastoral ministry. We don't really want to, but we know that we probably should.

Conversely, we also know that it is a major category of spiritual growth in the life of a disciple of Jesus. It is attributed to the great reformer Martin Luther that "there are three conversions . . . of the heart, the conversion of the mind, and the conversion of the purse." Charles Spurgeon writes, "With some Christians, the last part of their nature that ever gets sanctified is their pockets." The Scripture has plenty of places that talk about the importance of money and possessions in the life of a person of faith. And this deeply important teaching has nothing to do with church operational expenses.

It says that people who understand this and exhibit generosity are embracing "true life."

> Instruct those who are rich in the present age not to be arrogant or to set their hope on the uncertainty of wealth, but on God, who richly provides us with all things to enjoy. Instruct them to do what is good, to be rich in good works, to be generous and willing to share, storing up treasure for themselves as a good foundation for the coming age, so that they may take hold of what is truly life. (1 Tim. 6:17–19)

So, the capital campaign becomes simultaneously an opportunity to raise necessary funds and a way to see members of the congregation spiritually matured in somewhat unexpected ways.

Deepening Our Devotion

Jesus did not share the aversion to discussing money that many modern pastors and Christians have. It is widely known (and often forgotten) that He was rather quick to bring up the topic of money when asking probing questions about people's faith. I would love to take the time to explore the theological and practical implications of this. Suffice it to say that how one handles the financial resources God has provided for them is a significant barometer of their faith.

This is not to imply that people who give more money are "better Christians." But Jesus seemed to use the topic to get to the root of the matter. Why did He applaud the widow who gave 100 percent of everything she had? Why did He ask the rich man to sell everything and give his money away? It was likely because He knew that our faith is often marked by our tendency to either hold on white-knuckled to our stuff or open our hands and hearts to what God may have us do with His money.

So it is not recommended that church leaders say, "This campaign is not about the money, but about the spiritual growth we can all experience." It is not recommended because it is not true. The campaign is both about raising money for the church and about how that causes us to ask deep spiritual questions about our lives.

For churches that are accustomed to a common curriculum or church-wide study motif for adults, the campaign provides an excellent opportunity to use those platforms to teach about giving, generosity, sacrifice, a meaningful life, God's ownership of our resources, and more.

The common places for this to happen are:

- Groups
- Classes
- Bible Studies
- Leadership Meetings
- Worship Services
- Sermons
- Prayer Meetings
- Other . . .

Billy Graham said, "Give me five minutes with a person's checkbook and I will tell you where their heart is."[5] Campaigns can be a personal check-up on the checkbook (though no one seems to carry one anymore).

The idea still stands—the way we spend our money is inseparably linked to what we truly value. Jesus told us there was a connection like a spiritual cord between our bank account and our heart (Matt. 6:21).

Two Different Approaches

It is a major missed opportunity if the campaign skips the glaring opportunity for nurturing the congregation and gets reduced to a basic fundraising format. As we say at Auxano, there is nothing wrong with fundraising, but this is not what the church should be about when a massive opportunity to disciple people is served on a silver platter.

This is the **funding-only** format and is *not recommended*:

1. We need money for a very special project.
2. You should consider giving extra money because it is great for the church but we can't pay for it out of our operational funds.
3. Pray about this and then pledge or give.

An entirely different format allows for individuals, families, Sunday school classes and small groups to go on a spiritual journey. The narrative changes in beautiful ways. The **discipleship-then-funding** format goes like this:

1. Our church has the opportunity to increase our impact.
2. It is causing us all to think about what our lives are really about and do a self-evaluation on our level of generosity and openhandedness with God's resources entrusted to us.
3. Each of us should renew and review the powerful spiritual principles of generosity and how

a Christian can live a counter-cultural life in this world.

4. What if we committed again to live this amazing and abundant life as we join the chain of generous people of faith that have gone before us?
5. Could we be generous all the time, not just when there is a special project?
6. We could pray about giving above and beyond because God has gone above and beyond for us in the gospel of Jesus Christ.
7. What if we depended on God in a new way, stretching our faith and our generosity?
8. Consider a pledge or commitment to our church's capital campaign as an act of worship—recommitting to Jesus Christ, His kingdom, and our church's future.

Discipleship guru and capital fundraising colleague David Putman reminds us that anytime you are reprioritizing how you spend or utilize money to invest in the work of Christ, something simple but dramatic happens. He applies it to not just the campaigns he has led, but the ones he and his wife have personally participated in. "When I am thinking 'less of me and more of Jesus,' my faith and my generosity grows. That's why I think campaigns are power-packed with potential for spiritual growth and discipleship."[6]

QUESTIONS TO CONSIDER

Does our church make a distinction between stewardship and generosity? Tithing and offering? What other words do we use?

How would we rate ourselves in regard to teaching and development in generosity?

Are there discipleship venues or places where we could infuse teaching around generosity and giving?

Chapter Two

Three Conditions for Generosity

One of the primary questions I hear when churches are considering a capital campaign is, not surprisingly, "How much do you think we can raise at our church?" There are short answers to this question that follow a simple formula to arrive at a fairly accurate educated guess (we covered this in chapter 1). And there are longer and more nuanced ways to analyze this with more accuracy. But really there is a question before the question and it is this:

Do the conditions exist in a church
to have a highly effective campaign?

Let's face it. There are some times when it is easier to raise money in the church than others. And it does not mean that we can always raise funds in an ideal scenario. Sometimes, we just need to play the hand we are dealt.

The reality of any campaign environment is that there are a handful of factors both in our control and out of our control that have bearing on the fruit of a capital campaign. But, in general, there are certain conditions that have to be in the atmosphere for optimal outcomes in a faith-based capital campaign.

Those conditions are:

Trust in Leadership
Clear and Compelling Vision
Sense That We Are Winning

Trust in Leadership

If a church has a good track record of operating with integrity, this condition is met. Sometimes, however, the current leadership may be dealing with financial mishaps or mishandling in the past. In this case, a bit more effort needs to be made going forward to operate with an open book and highly communicative approach to the money handling aspect of church life. Reporting and awareness are always a good idea, but especially in a church with some smudges on their record.

With the public awareness of money chicanery by churches, religious organizations, and non-profits, it is a fair question to ask, "Are the leaders at our church acting in a trustworthy manner? Do I have a sense that they do what they say when it comes to management of money?"

When it comes to voluntary giving, people are making a trust decision. Once they release control of resources, they really have little to do with how it is handled.

Trust tends to come from a long reputation of open communication about decisions regarding money and other aspects of church life. Consider the following passages from both Old and New Testaments that allude to the idea that trustworthiness is a characteristic of a spiritual person or leader.

> "Whoever is faithful in very little is also faithful in much, and whoever is unrighteous in very little is also unrighteous in much. So if you have not been faithful with worldly wealth, who will trust you with what is genuine? And if you have not been faithful with what belongs to someone else, who will give you what is your own?" (Luke 16:10–12)

> "But you should select from all the people able men, God-fearing, trustworthy, and hating dishonest profit. Place them over the people as commanders of thousands, hundreds, fifties, and tens." (Exod. 18:21)

Many of us in church leadership have a sober sense that this is important. We have heard about or experienced both the power of trust and the paralysis of mistrust.

In the introduction to the book *The Speed of Trust: The One Thing That Changes Everything*, author Stephen Covey writes:

> There is one thing that is common to every individual, relationship, team, family, organization, nation, economy, and civilization throughout the world—one thing which, if removed, will destroy the most powerful government, the most successful business, the most thriving economy, the most influential leadership, the greatest friendship, the strongest character, the deepest love . . . that one thing is trust.[7]

Tina Jepson writes in a blog published by CauseVox that there are five critical ways to build and maintain trust with those who are financially supporting an organization like the church:

1. Keep the Message Clear and Consistent
2. Be Up-Front about Your Financials
3. Regularly Report on Results
4. Don't Be Pushy
5. Show Your Appreciation[8]

Questions to Consider and Discuss

Is there anything we need to be concerned about regarding trust levels?

If you were estimating the trust level the congregation has in church leadership on a scale of 1 to 10 where 1 represented broken or almost nonexistent trust and 10 represented the highest level you can expect or imagine, where would you rank the trust level at your church in the following categories?

Financial Integrity: ______

Decision Making: ______

Communication: ______

Follow-Through: ______

Which of these statements best characterizes your church and why?

____ There is no systematic pattern of reporting on use of finances.

____ We report budgets and spending but rarely connect that with mission or progress as a ministry.

____ People are generally aware that we are doing well with finances but not because of a proactive approach to reporting. They know that if there is a "problem," we will inform them.

____ People know that if they want information, they can ask for it. We have an "open book" policy.

____ We have a regular pattern of connecting people's giving and investment with mission results.

Is there anything we should start, stop, or continue in regard to the kind of openness that is required to build and keep trust?

Start	Stop	Continue

Figure 2.1

Clear and Compelling Vision

In addition to solid trust in leaders, another key to developing increased giving in the church is continual clarity about the overall mission of the church. Before people will be excited to fund a particular project, they need to understand how that project supports the ministry or mission aim of the church.

As obvious as this may seem, many churches operate with muddy vision for the future. And as time passes, people are becoming more skeptical about a "bigger is better" mentality about capital investment—particularly facilities.

Depending on the context, there may even be hesitancy about a campaign because of the perceived difference between what a church "needs" to do the ministry effectively, and what church leadership "wants" for any number of reasons.

It is a commonly understood and repeated phrase that "people won't just give money to bricks and mortar." This is repeated as a way to highlight the need for a vision-based explanation. But there is more to that story than the quip reveals.

Sometimes a church has an *indirect connection* to vision. For instance, a debt retirement campaign may not (on the surface) look like it is vision-based. And yet, it can be—or should be—right? It is the responsibility of the leadership to articulate the connections to vision with "if, then" statements like: "If we retire the debt, it frees up cash flow that we have wanted to invest in our ministry to the poor in our region."

Idlewild Baptist Church in Lutz, Florida, is one of the largest Southern Baptist Churches in the country. As they geared up for a capital campaign, they had dreams to use funding to plant churches and expand their children and student programs. Through a Congregational Assessment, they discerned that the congregation was passionately in favor of paying off the last $14M of the debt on their $100M facilities and grounds before investing in any further endeavors.

Being free from debt is not a vision even though it is a very good thing. They ran a capital campaign called "ACCELERATE" and clearly and compellingly communicated the indirect connections with vision. The main narrative of their campaign was the excitement of how they will be able to fuel the vision for new churches and children and student initiatives with the money they save each year not having to pay down a mortgage.

A **direct connection** to vision is when the church states that their desired future is to plant three churches in the next three years and the money being raised goes directly to fund that idea. Or if the vision is to reach younger families—so the church is building a family center or renovating the youth wing—then that connection to vision seems to be more direct than indirect.

First Reformed Church is in New Jersey and was an established church before the United States even became a country. Their historic church is exactly at the center of a pre-Revolution town in the Northeast. The fellowship hall is a multi-purpose space that is by far the most utilized square footage on their campus for both church meetings and community gatherings as it is directly across from city hall. Their campaign to renovate, expand, and modernize "Friendship Hall" was a direct connection to their long-term vision to become the *intersection of faith and life for the city.*

The point is this: **The best condition for cultivating generosity is when people hear the vision and it is so compelling that the logical next step is to fund that vision.**

Questions to Consider

If we selected a member randomly and asked them about the vision of the church, what would he or she say?

Do we have direct or indirect connections between the project or projects and the direction our church is headed?

How would you rate your project/s on a "link to vision" continuum? (See Figure 2.2.)

Which project or projects will be the hardest to get people excited about and why?

Project Continuum	
PROJECT NAME	LINK TO VISION DIRECT ◀ - ▶ INDIRECT

Figure 2.2

Sense That We Are Winning

At a very basic level, people want to invest in a winner. This may sound unspiritual or crass, but it is true. There are many reasons for this. A common-sense principle like "Don't throw good money after bad" is often in people's minds.

Technically, God is the one that allows a church to have a sense of "winning" or being blessed with results. A better way to say this probably is that we have a "sense that God is at work in a visible way." The spiritual notion (made popular by author Henry Blackaby in *Experiencing God*) is that we should "look for where God is already at work and join Him there."

Add to this that the modern advisor or wealth manager will coach their clients to be savvy about charitable contributions and vet the places to which they give.

I had a significant investor call me on the phone at the church where I was working to ask whether or not the pastor was being overpaid. He was embarrassed, in a sense, to make the phone call. But his financial advisor was pressing him by saying, "You are giving a lot of money to this church—are you sure someone isn't abusing the funds in some way?"

Whether a basic economic instinct, spiritual sensitivity, or the educated donor checking up on the church—the truth is that people will feel emotionally better about investing in something that is showing signs of effectiveness. As church leaders, we cannot assume that people are being stingy or petty when asking themselves (or asking us) questions about spending. Maybe they are being good managers of the money God has entrusted to them.

High capacity and high-net-worth people in our churches are faced with many opportunities to invest in God's work, so they will be the first to ask themselves or their leaders:

> "Are we headed in the right direction? Are things going well? Are we raising money because it will help an already effective ministry?"

It is a stewardship issue for them (and for all of us). With the money God is asking them to manage for His purposes, is the church capital campaign something into which they should pour those resources?

Questions to Consider

What are the ways we can see God's work in and through our church? List the things that are working effectively below:

Is there a common awareness of this? Are signs of God's work through our church celebrated or reported regularly? How?

How can we cultivate a sense of awareness about spiritual and missional victories through our church on a more regular basis (whether we are conducting a capital campaign or not)?

Chapter Three

Three Threats to a Successful Campaign

I have been directly involved with many campaigns and in virtually every case, the project gets all the attention. What I mean is that there is a perceived need or desired upgrade that gets discussed long before the hard work of capital campaign readiness is employed.

Senior leaders of churches often have ideas about projects that are connected to ministry. But it seems like the cart is almost always ahead of the horse. Vision clarity is a secondary consideration at best. And that's a problem, because ultimately people give to vision. And if vision is unclear, we have our work cut out for us.

Think about this scenario:

- Leaders have a dream for an expansion, addition, or renovation
- Leaders quickly realize that it will not become a reality unless it is connected with ministry effectiveness

- Leaders shoehorn the idea into the church's strategic direction

This is an exaggeration and a bit unfair, some may say. But I have seen this in the churches I have served more times than I care to recount.

Campaigns allow us to fuel vision. Buildings are tools to fulfill mission and ministry dreams. Clarity about the future will naturally produce the question, "What are we going to need to allow that future to become a reality?"

Vision should always be the horse,
and campaigns should always be the cart.

A campaign is not a mission, and a building is not a vision.

This is one threat among many that jeopardize a church's short-term and long-term health and success.

The threats to a successful campaign are primarily in three categories:

Overpromise and Underdeliver
Campaign without Help
Microwave Process

Overpromise and Underdeliver

There is a temptation to drum up support, excitement, and financial giving by creating a Taj Mahal level project to create a wow-factor for your congregation. The mistake here is to say, "Look at this amazing project!" and create an expectation that cannot be met without putting the church in significant financial jeopardy.

Most of the men and women that I have met in church leadership are committed to God and their church and are trying to do the right thing. I have never sensed anyone trying to be intentionally careless in the management of the church's future. But there is a strong tendency to succumb to the threat of an overpromise.

A few years ago, I worked with a church in Ohio that had dreamed about renovation and expansion. After a study of their congregation, we determined that the church could raise capital in the amount of approximately $1.5M.

The problem was that a building committee led by an ambitious and optimistic chairman had developed a $12M dream. As frustrated as the leadership was (even with my assessment of their capacity), I sat with the pastor recently, and he is still incredibly relieved that he didn't lead the church into a disaster that could have had generational repercussions.

As leaders, we want to motivate and inspire our people. And being conservative or "not biting off more than we can chew" doesn't sound as motivational as "Who wouldn't want an expansion that looks like this?!"

The threat to success here is a loss of credibility or trust—and a need to go back and redesign or reduce scope and then take the time to explain why what we are now getting is different from the concept we first "sold" to the congregation.

Campaign without Help

At the risk of appearing to be a consultant writing a paragraph about how consultants are so wonderful, let me clarify: I do not think that every church needs a strategic outsider. But many do.

Without process and accountability, the smartest and most capable people in the world will struggle to complete a campaign in a timely manner. I liken it to the popularity of weight loss, fitness, or recovery programs where the knowledge of "what to do" is not the hardest part of the equation. Having the accountability of a process, system, and ultimately another human being (a coach) will breed success at a much higher frequency.

The senior pastor rarely has extra time to devote to a large-scale capital campaign (and unless he or she has done one before, they do not have the expertise either). The staff is busy each day meeting ministry demands. And our best lay people are running businesses, raising families, teaching classes, practicing law, and everything else you can imagine. Who is going to keep this thing on track?

The threat to success here is that *not considering help* may end up wasting kingdom resources in the end. It is a little bit like trying to remodel your kitchen. You may know how to do it (or like me, you know enough to be dangerous) but end up spending more money on lost efficiency, and often call the building contractor eventually anyway.

An important note is George Barna's discovery that churches using reputable capital campaign consultants raise 50 percent more than churches who do not. Even if that statistic is half wrong, how much would an additional 25 percent mean to your church's future?

Microwave Process

In addition to the threats of overpromising or "going it alone" is the equally powerful threat of trying to rush through a campaign or get it up and down as quickly as possible because we are either impatient or uncomfortable.

Visionary leaders can often see the future already in their mind's eye. Slowing down to take a large group of people through a thoughtful process to gain ownership and spiritual momentum can be enormously frustrating to leaders who wish everyone saw things the way they do. And you can't blame them. They have likely given more thought and prayer to these ideas and projects than almost everyone.

At the same time, rushing or "microwaving" a fundraising process misses out on the opportunity to do some Vision Clarity Clean-Up (if that is necessary) and some Generosity Discipleship (where many churches are underdeveloped).

Consider this very direct article by Will Mancini. He doesn't pull any punches when it comes to his passion for a thorough sense of vision clarity as the foundation for this discussion—and the basis for most missteps:

Typical Campaigns Promote Anorexic Vision

Standard campaigns are driven by a weak vision, not a healthy one. It all starts when the consultant wrongly validates the goals of the campaign—land acquisition, or building, or debt reduction, or multi-site expansion—*as the church's vision*. Sure, you need to clarify what you want to buy. But capital needs like these, by themselves, don't convey the substance and sustainability of a *well-articulated vision*. The campaign goal is not the vision, but a piece of a large whole. And capital campaign consultants are not equipped, or motivated to help you articulate the larger whole.

Think about what a pastor unknowingly does to his congregation—it's like trying to run a marathon on junk food. A pastor asks people to sacrifice (marathon training) and then feeds them French fries (we are going to be a multi-site church). May I ask you a blunt question? Who really cares about a multi-site strategy? Isn't that a means to some greater end? Why would people care about the means unless you unpack the bigger picture and the deeper motives behind multi-site? And, by the way, if you justify your vision with a phrase like "we want to reach, teach, and release disciples of Jesus," or some other 3-phrase mantra, that isn't enough.

What have the "canned-approach guys" done to adapt over the last few years? Rather than clarifying the bigger vision, consultants encourage you to tack on a missional initiative or feel-good project to "compensate" for the capital need. For example, let's say building expansion is going to cost two million dollars. The pastor begins wiggling in his seat because he anticipates some pushback regarding the facility expense, especially from the millennial generation. Rather than exploring and developing clearly the facility's role in the bigger vision, the consultant recommends including money for the medical facility in Togo. Does that sound heroic? Well it may be, but not if it is "covering up" a lack of vision for the building to begin with.

What's the answer? Yes, you want to rally your people to a better future. And yes, that better future may involve sacrificial giving. But do you think a few polished sermons, a cool building elevation, and a nifty vision mantra is enough? People need—and deserve—more than a general sense of your church's future if you expect them to sacrifice. *They need something vividly clear and stunningly compelling all centered in God's unique work through your church.*

You don't know what you don't know? The impact of the campaign industry is so widespread, pastors are truly unaware of how underfed their congregations are with vision junk food. Hence this post title—Is it possible that your last campaign actually hurt your church? What if there was a way for vision to be so clear that the campaign felt altogether different, completely better and totally natural? You don't know what you don't know. When most churches start a campaign, they are usually a good six months away from the clarity they really need to drive it. An under-developed vision always leads to under-realized resourcing.[9]

Questions to Consider

Is there a burning need for the project we are considering or is it "nice to have," causing us to do some "spinning" the way we explain the opportunities?

What is the burning answer to "why" in just one sentence? Practice writing it here in your own words:

Do we have assumptions about the people of our congregation? What does our congregation know, understand, and embrace about our dreams for the future?

Can we name the handful of people in addition to the senior pastor that will bear the weight of campaign responsibility whether we have a consultant/coach or not?

Have we utilized a consultant in the past? Why or why not? Do we have a sense for what this would cost compared to the workload?

Chapter Four

Three Baseline Planning Tools

There are a few things that are nonnegotiable when it comes to being clear about the campaign. It is hard to imagine a campaign without a clear explanation that informs about the elements of the capital project or projects, answers people's primary questions, and declares a timeline of how the campaign will be conducted.

Any campaign I have ever done begins with three basic tools or documents that get everything started and make the process feel official. These are the documents before all other documents—the foundational ones from which everything else will emanate.

Every subsequent media piece, event, gathering, or message will find its direction from these documents that are primarily meant to be internal guiding documents but are critically important to the success of the campaign.

Those tools are:

Case for Support

Frequently Asked Questions

Campaign Calendar

Case for Support

Some would call this the Campaign Vision or the Project Vision. It is a "white paper" that describes the project in a manner that helps people understand its nature, features, and importance to the church. Calling it a Case for Support implies that we are shaping a narrative that builds a case that will motivate people to consider financially supporting our desired outcome.

By answering these questions, we are on the way to developing our Case for Support: *What are we doing? Why are we investing in this? How will it change things?*

What are we doing?

The answer to the first question of "what" is the description at a high level of what we hope to invest money in that requires more than the current operational funds will allow. To some leaders, the project or projects seem patently obvious. But to many people who aren't thinking about the leadership of the church every day, they may not even understand.

For people to grasp the magnitude and importance, there also needs to be a cost (or at least a possible range of cost) associated with the features of the project or projects as well as narrative (a paragraph or two) to describe the project.

For instance, if I were at your church, my level of buy-in would be related to my perception of the need or impact of the project when it is completed. But equally as powerful is my perception of the return on the investment—does it seem like a "good deal" to me? If we wanted a new ladies' bathroom, for instance, there would likely be a lot of support because of its practicality. What if we said that because of complications to our plumbing system and its expansion, the ladies' bathroom will cost a half million dollars?

That may change some people's minds about what at first glance was a "no-brainer."

Here are some examples of short but meaningful explanations that a church could use along with the price as articulated by a range:

Renovate Children's Wing ($500,000–600,000): With so many young families joining our church, we see potential for even more to do so. Adding four new classrooms and a play area to the west side of our building will provide more space for Sunday programming as well as provide opportunities throughout the week for activities that bring people together and into our building. The Children's Wing has not been updated since the 1980s, so we believe now is the time to capitalize on the opportunity to reach young families moving into our area.

Update Sanctuary ($800,000–$1,000,000): As the center of communal life for our congregation, the sanctuary is a key environment for us to communicate the importance of worship and the importance of life together. We have been struggling for a while with the sound system not working well and we are desperately in need of updating décor—including carpet, painting the walls, and some refurbishing of the pews. The platform area will be expanded as we have both a traditional choir and worship teams that all share that space as they lead us each Sunday.

Buy Property for Relocation ($1.5M–$2M): We knew when our church started ten years ago that this exciting day would arrive. We have outgrown the school we are renting and need a permanent facility for our congregation. Our real estate advisors have secured a few parcels for us to consider—each of them could suit our needs. We are raising the necessary funds to secure property so that we can begin to make plans to build on that property as soon as funding will allow.

Why are we investing in this?

The first question of "what" basically explains the project—is it an expansion, renovation, or relocation, and how big, how much, etc. The answer to the second question of "why" will address the ministry reason or the vision-connected reason to invest this money. Somehow, the importance and urgency of completing the project needs be clear, or the consequences of not doing the campaign need to be evident (without being negative or threatening).

If the examples above represent the kind of narrative that creates a top-level understanding of what we are trying to accomplish, another batch of writing can address the vision-based answer to what this is all about. In other words, the reasons need to be stated to answer the why questions.

For example, consider this as a way to bullet-list reasons.

We are excited about what God is doing in and through us but know that there is more for us to experience and accomplish. Our church's vision to reach our community with God's love and increase our impact is driving our desire to invest in these projects. Completing them will help us:

- Create a more welcoming space for the people that come to our church
- Communicate to young families that we have them in mind and created a space for them
- Improve our worship environment to the excellence that matches our passion for God
- Have the necessary instruction environments to teach people about the faith so they can live it out when they are in the community

You are likely thinking this way already. List some of the reasons the leadership of your church has been dreaming about and planning for capital projects:

1. ______________________________

2. ______________________________

3. ______________________________

4. ______________________________

How will it change things?

This is the place where the church's vision for the future and the capital campaign collide. This is why a clear understanding of a picture of the future of the church is extremely important. Clarity of vision is everything.

Most churches that ask us about raising capital have done less with visioning than they have with building plans. A lot less. This is not meant to be a scathing critique but rather a reality check. It is actually quite normal. But it is also necessary to add this into the ingredients at some point before the campaign begins.

I have officiated a number of weddings over the years and have seen a shift in priority when it comes to how money is spent. Churches getting excited about building plans but not having a clear vision for the future is the relational equivalent to young couples spending tens of thousands on their wedding day but ten minutes on their pre-marital counseling. In many areas of life, really good people can unintentionally slip into imbalanced priorities.

Casting a clear vision is one of the single most important best practices when it comes to creating a picture of the church's future in a compelling way. And connecting the projects with that clear vision is true north for campaigns—it is what everyone should be shooting for. Ultimately, I believe a capital campaign should be classified in the category of change management. Taking a group from point A to point Z is a process of communicating the reasons and urgency for change.

This rings particularly true for me when I review the work of Dr. John Kotter in regard to organizational change. Kotter's classic work on change management reminds us of the key steps in managing change.[10] The wording may need to be somewhat adapted, but much of Kotter's eight actions apply to a church-wide capital campaign.

Key Steps to Managing Change

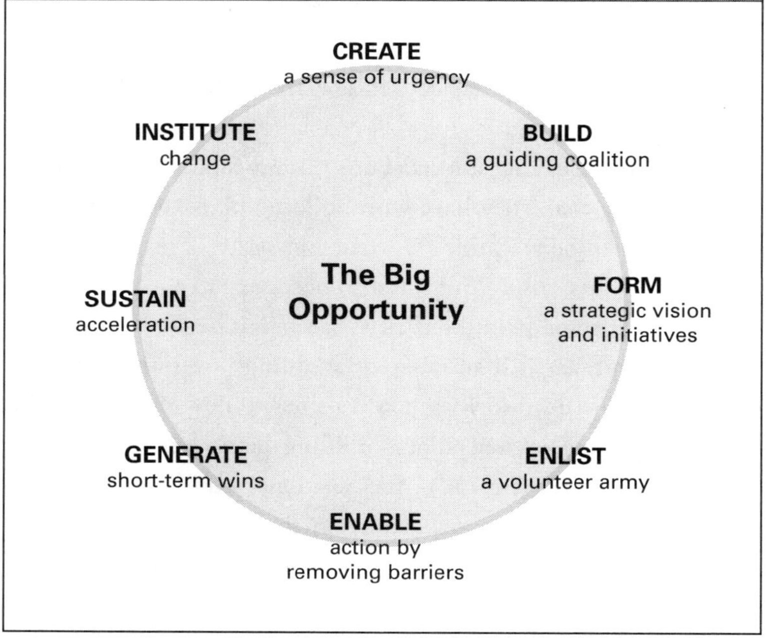

Figure 4.1

Because I believe a capital campaign marks a significant "chapter turn" in the life of a church, I think about it as this journey that Kotter describes. When I am helping churches begin to form their vision, I am looking for where the urgency lies and how we can begin to shape the narrative that the congregation will soon hear. I am also trying to ready the pastor and leadership for the possible emotional reactions they may encounter. By likening a campaign to a major church change, they understand the posture with which they can approach people who may be getting agitated.

Questions to Consider

What is driving the timing of your current dreams about a project or projects that lie ahead? Why is now the best time compared to waiting, say, for a year or two? If you were rating your project or projects on an urgency scale of 1 ("We would prefer to do this but can wait if we must") and 10 ("We will move heaven and earth to get this done"), what would each one rate?

What do we risk missing out on if we don't strike soon? Lost opportunity? Is there an obvious "next step" for the church presenting itself to us right now?

What are ways to communicate the sense of urgency? How will a successful campaign change the church in a positive way in terms of ministry and mission?

List the positive benefits to ministry:

1. ______________________________

2. ______________________________

3. ______________________________

4. ______________________________

Frequently Asked Questions

This is absolutely my favorite and most recommended approach to communicating with clarity. Using the question-and-answer format gets right to the heart of the matter. Frequently Asked Questions is a fairly common feature of websites and written communication for many churches and organizations.

This method is succinct and addresses many of the questions people have asked or concerns they have expressed. Instead of avoiding those questions and hoping they go away, we can take a proactive approach. In so doing, we show that we are operating with openness and integrity—we are not trying to sweep under the rug the inevitable challenges that come along with any major initiative.

In the churches where we have conducted a Congregational Assessment, the surveys and interviews allow people to reveal their questions and concerns. That becomes the source material from which we can formulate the church's communication strategy. Congregations will tell you how to walk them through a campaign if you will let them. Creating the pre-campaign feedback loop is enormously helpful to the overall success.

Categories that are often included in an FAQ:

Current State of Church and Its Ministries

Vision for the Future
Project or Projects Being Funded by the Campaign
The Discipleship Aspect of Our Journey Together
The Practical Side of Giving and Pledging

Here are examples for each:

Current State of Church and Its Ministries

Is our church growing? Yes—in very exciting ways. Many churches in America are seeing a slowing of growth in worship services and less frequent attendance by even the most faithful. But not only are we holding steady in worship right now, there is much more to the story. What we are experiencing is unprecedented growth—more middle school and high school students at camp and being baptized, record-breaking Vacation Bible School attendance, more adults than ever serving the under-served in our region and more. Almost every measure that focuses on discipleship and mobilization of our people for the sake of God's kingdom is higher than ever.

Vision for the Future

How did we arrive at the decision to have a capital campaign? Our vision for the next five years is to double our discipleship groups and continue to have recovery groups and local clubs use our property on a daily basis. Additionally, the property team has been generating a list of repairs needed across our campus that fall outside the scope of the operating budget. The church board feels so strongly that God is already showing us that our impact is increasing and will continue. Since we are in a strategic location directly across from the town hall and on the turnpike, we want to not only make repairs, but also expand our fellowship hall since it is the center of church and community life these days! We are preparing for what is next and believe that time is of the essence.

Project or Projects Being Funded by the Campaign

What is driving the need to expand the sanctuary? Our property analysis team has been interacting with architects and touring other churches to try and address the crowding challenges we currently have. Their desire was to do this in the most economical way that still held true to the design style of our building. Many alternatives were considered and we heard feedback from the worship committee and other members. Over a period of months of deliberation and prayer, we believe the design is what will allow more people to meet each other and meet God in a special way in worship. After all, our worship service is the center of our church life and the expansion allows for 30 percent more attenders (200 people per service).

The Discipleship Aspect of Our Journey

How will I know what to give? What amount is appropriate? This is between you and God (and your spouse if you are married). Our campaign is a time of self-reflection and prayer as we ask God, "How can I reflect my commitment to You through my giving and living?" Our next few months can be a time of remembrance and gratitude as we each think back over God's faithfulness to us as individuals and a church. As we consider ways to rearrange or rethink our spending or the use of our accumulated assets, it becomes a truly spiritual journey. God does not need money nor force us to give it away. At the same time, we can respond in gratitude. We can also remember the truth that it all belongs to God anyway.

The Practical Side of Giving and Pledging

What if we do not reach our target amount in three-year pledges? First, it is our firm belief that we will meet our target—perhaps even exceed it. In the event we do not, we will decide as a congregation how to best utilize the funds, keeping in mind the priorities that have been decided on by the congregation and the leadership. The financial strength and stability of the church always receives the highest consideration in planning for how we proceed.

Brainstorm

Can you think of some questions that have already been asked that should be included in your church's campaign FAQ?

List them here:

Can you anticipate questions (because you know the people and culture of your congregation) that haven't been asked yet but will likely come up?

List them here:

Campaign Calendar

As simple as this sounds when it comes to planning, it should be noted that starting with a campaign calendar as one of the foundational documents is a must. Creating a "draft calendar" internally may take a few days. But it is nonnegotiable to ensure that this calendar is distributed to staff and leadership a few weeks ahead of the first date on the calendar. This allows for time to make adjustments and for people on the staff and in the ministries of the church to know that something is coming that will interrupt the normal flow of church life. This also delivers good information and breeds internal ownership at just the right time.

Again, the best-practice principle here is that we don't try to insert a church-wide capital campaign into a busy calendar or lump it on top of the fullness of church life. Something has to be suspended or canceled (hard-to-swallow in churches) so that the campaign takes preeminence.

There are many ways to format a campaign calendar, of course. But to model one way to look at this, consider the following line-list style for a six- to seven-month approach:

Discover

Vision Clarifying	July 20
Compile Costs, Designs, Due Diligence	August 1
Campaign Executive Team Orientation	August 15
Draft Case, FAQ, Calendar	September 1

Discover (as described in chapter 1) is the time period where church leadership is primarily the group doing the research, investigation, analysis, and initial draft of the narrative in a Case for Support statement. This phase provides the foundation for everything to follow and requires that the campaign get very clear in its purpose and focus before we start to craft the way it will be communicated widely.

Design

Plan and Design Approach to Worship	September 1
Decide on Discipleship Elements	September 15
Plan and Design Meetings and Gatherings	September 30
Decide on Theme, Brand, Title	October 5
Decide on Communications/Media Deliverables	October 12

Once we have a strong sense of the focus of the campaign, we can start to craft a way to communicate it with our congregation and our culture in mind. This asks the questions like, "Can we include campaign elements in the ways and places people already gather?" or "What event or meeting should we create that will allow people to be informed and inspired?"

This phase starts to include more people in the conversation as we will want to talk to those who lead the areas of communications, worship, and groups/classes.

Disciple

Leader Orientation	November 15
Campaign Team Training	January 10
Campaign Team Training	February 5
Launch Sunday/Weekend in Worship	February 20
Small Groups Begin Curriculum	February 20
Events and Gatherings Begin	February 21
Campaign Elements/Teaching in Worship	February 27
Campaign Elements/Teaching in Worship	March 4
Campaign Elements/Teaching in Worship	March 11
Campaign Elements/Teaching in Worship	March 18
Commitment/Pledge Sunday	March 25
Celebration Sunday	April 3

This section of the calendar starts to include many people. Churches will often have both staff and volunteer leaders as the campaign leaders of various areas or teams. We then include others, recruited for both their contribution of help to the campaign, but also because they will be more likely to take ownership of the campaign and its results. Ownership precedes funding. These will be some of the most supportive members of the church financially as well.

Questions to Consider

When does it seem best to conduct the public phase of our campaign? Identify the worship services during which we "go public" with our plans and requests for financial support.

What are some of the currently existing meetings into which we could insert campaign teaching (information and inspiration)?

If the campaign was in three basic phases (Discover, Design, Disciple), where in the church calendar do these generally seem to fit? (See Figure 1.9 on page 19.)

Three Basic Phases – Calendar Planning				
	Q1	**Q2**	**Q3**	**Q4**
DISCOVER				
DESIGN				
DISCIPLE				

Figure 4.2

Chapter Five

Three Kinds of Campaign Teams

For the last few decades of church capital campaigns, a very common occurrence is the use of campaign teams. There are two primary reasons for this: **extra help and wider ownership**.

What this means is that a church (especially church staff) is already very busy, so during a church-wide initiative the size of a campaign, there is a need for more hands-on-deck. Getting many people involved adds horsepower but it also increases the likelihood that people will care about and "own" the church's future and the campaign's success.

The point is not that the church staff is busy and lay people are not. Campaign teams follow the "many hands make light work" principle and allow core members of the church (who will be the key funders of the campaign) to be on the inside track. People fund what they help create.

Charlie Koopman of Oak Pointe Church in Michigan reminds us that keeping the staff involved in the campaign is critical since they have so much influence on members of the congregation.

"We involve our staff because they shouldn't be in the dark. We also know that they have given their lives to this ministry and will want to be at the head of the spear when it comes to leading the congregation, answering questions, and advocating for the campaign."

For years, Auxano has shared these Keys to Great Campaign Teams:

1. Each team should have multiple leaders.
2. Most teams should have five to ten total members.
3. Each team should enlist a team of helpers for special events.
4. Enlist people who have a positive attitude toward the campaign.
5. Clear all people through the Campaign Team Leader first.
6. Enlist couples together to serve on one team.
7. Set expectations of each member spending five to ten hours a month.
8. Goal of the team is to recruit 50 percent experienced leaders and 50 percent new leaders.

Some common examples of teams fit into three categories:

Planning Teams

Spiritual Life Teams

Gatherings Teams

Planning Teams

Administrative

This team or person is the connection point between the pastor, consultant, church office, and campaign team. This person will assist the consultant and other team leaders with the administrative detail of mailing and membership lists for the purpose of recruiting and inviting throughout the campaign.

Communications and Media

This person, team, or staff is ultimately responsible for the media and communications deliverables throughout the campaign. The team is almost always dictated by the size of the church and whether or not they have dedicated staff for media and communications. If not, there still needs to be a person or group that manages volunteers and outside vendors.

Senior Pastor and Senior Level Staff

The senior pastor (and other senior staff) become the chief communicators for the capital projects through personal support, team member recruiting, and public vision casting. They can delegate much of the campaign preparation but usually will influence direction at a conceptual level to get things started. Then, the senior pastor will jump back in during the public phase, attending meetings, preaching sermons, etc.

Follow Up and Finances

This person (often the financial administrator of the church) will privately and professionally aid the process of pledge recording and reporting. Then this person or a team will plan a multi-year strategy of consistent communication regarding the campaign project to both pledgers and givers, as well as yet-to-give households and new members.

Spiritual Life Teams

Worship Planning

This is a person or group that strategizes with the campaign team, allowing for campaign-related ideas and communication to have a place in the church services. From a staff perspective, this is often a worship leader or music minister that does much of the worship service planning, but it can include others as well.

Discipleship, Groups, and Spiritual Formation Leaders

Depending on the church, this can be a combination of staff and other leaders who focus their efforts on the spiritual maturity of the congregation. These leaders can help think through ways to engage the adults in discipleship and teaching opportunities around generosity. Churches call it different things—small groups, Sunday school classes, discipleship groups—but this refers to the way we gather people to spiritually develop them in our context.

Prayer

For many churches, a critical component of day-to-day church life involves prayer—prayer teams, prayer meetings, and more. This can be parlayed into our campaign spiritual focus. At the same time, a church can create or develop a prayer event, team, or emphasis with the campaign that may have a life after the campaign is over.

Age Graded and Age Appropriate

There are often both staff and volunteer leaders that tend to our children and youth on a regular basis. The campaign can be a great opportunity to allow for both the church's vision as well as the church's teaching about generosity to be delivered in age-graded ways. A team can decide what those ways will be and then make sure there are people trained to deliver this messaging.

Gatherings Teams

Large Events

A team of individuals can plan, recruit, design, and execute some events or large gatherings for the church campaign. This is a time outside of worship for fellowship, questions and answers, food, and inspiration. It is often part of campaign design in that it allows for people to have a more focused time of understanding what is at stake and hearing the case for supporting the campaign as it is tied to the future vision for the church.

Small or Home Gatherings

These households are willing to invite people to a home party where they will supply food and encouragement to fellow church members by speaking positively about the campaign goals. There is something special and powerful about a meeting of like-minded financial peers discussing the campaign with the pastor and graciously challenging each other to be positive and engaged in the giving process.

Leadership Gift Strategy

The campaign directors will, along with the senior pastor and consultant, determine a major gift strategy as well as an advanced pledge event for the campaign team and other leaders in the congregation. This may involve one-on-one meetings with potential lead givers or major donors (see chapter 10 "Considerations for Major Donors") and is based on the idea that God gives some to the church to encourage others by leading the way with their giving.

Questions to Consider

Which of the teams listed in this chapter will work best in our church culture? Do all of them work?

Have we utilized teams for something like this before like a previous campaign or large church-wide endeavor? How did it go?

Is there a certain idiosyncrasy of our church that demands we invent a new kind of campaign team not listed? What is it?

List the key leader or leaders (staff or other) that would likely shoulder responsibility for each of these areas—be sure to brainstorm at least one name for each team:

Administrative ______________________________

Communications ______________________________

Senior Staff ______________________________

Follow Up and Finances ______________________________

Worship Planning ______________________________

Discipleship, SS, Groups ______________________

Prayer ______________________

Children ______________________

Students ______________________

Large Events ______________________

Small or Home Gatherings ______________________

Leadership Giving ______________________

Custom Team ______________________

Chapter Six

Three Roles for Senior Pastors

As much as we create teams and spread the work load of a campaign, we have to face the reality that the senior pastor's energy will be tested. If executed well, many senior leaders find these times to be both exhilarating and exhausting.

Back in my days with Cargill, we used to refer to the spiritual excitement and increase of funds in a church during this time with a half-joke, teasing that "most of our pastors think they should do a campaign every couple of years whether they need the money or not." In reality, most senior pastors burn the candle at both ends during a campaign. While a church should do everything it can to off-load tasks from the pastor's to-do list, it is not realistic to believe that everything can be delegated, so a higher energy burn will be required of the senior pastor during a campaign.

Without exception, the most visible and vocal leader of the church has a crucial role or set of tasks during a campaign of this magnitude. He or she is adding meetings, appointments, writing, and a few other things to an already full calendar.

This is not meant to scare senior pastors who are reading this. It is a heads-up as you prepare. Then again, if you have been part of a capital campaign before, you probably could have written this chapter. This is not your first rodeo. The reason this explanation is included in this book is that most consultants are asked the question "What are the implications of this campaign for our pastor?" The campaign is a time of intensity for the pastor.

For many or most campaigns, senior pastors need to consider their role as:

Vision Caster
Preacher
Participant

Vision Caster

Many people will own the vision of the church and the connections that long-range view has with the campaign projects. The senior pastor, however, will be the primary carrier of that vision. This applies to the preaching, the meetings with members of the congregation, appearances at events and gatherings and even casual conversations.

When we recount that people ultimately "give to vision, not to bricks and mortar," we are primarily reminding folks that, as excited as they may be about a new building or renovation, we need to keep people's focus on the reason for all of this. When people like asking questions and hearing details about the projects, that is a good thing. And when staff and volunteers are able to answer those questions, show renderings or satisfy the congregation's curiosity, that is also good.

However, the senior pastor will be the one person that will hold us as a congregation to the discipline of remembering that capital campaigns are not our church's vision, and buildings and renovation projects are not our main ministry or mission.

Ronnie Floyd encourages pastors to be clear and concise:

> Yes, you have to go deep and comprehend the details so you know you understand the vision; however, when you cast it before others, they just need to know the work is already done. You need to be on top of it, but remember you are breaking it down, not only so others can grasp it, but also for them to be able to communicate it to others. It is not about how much you share, but share enough for the people to have complete clarity.[11]

Author Eric Swanson points us back to Steven Covey who wrote, "All things are created twice." Swanson goes on to explain:

> First there is the mental creation and then the physical creation. Vision pertains to this first creation. We have to see it before we can shape it into reality. From a Christian perspective, vision is the ability to clearly see and articulate where God wants us to go or what God wants us to do in a given situation. Vision is the bridge between present and future reality. As one man stated, "If you want to find a needle in a haystack it is almost impossible. Yet if you place a magnet on the edge of the haystack, the needles jump out." Vision is that magnet that attracts followers and resources.[12]

Preacher

Since the focal point of most churches is the worship service, preaching is one of the primary platforms to inform and inspire. The messages during the public phase of the campaign do not necessarily need to be about generosity and giving, but preachers should not ignore that teaching either. This becomes a great opportunity whether or not your church is underdeveloped in terms of the frequency of generosity messages.

The reason that preaching is so important during the campaign is that it gives the congregation the opportunity to hear a "state of the church" as well as the long-term vision for the future. Presenting a biblical approach to a life of generosity and sacrifice is critical to moving people forward in the journey toward spiritual maturity.

If a pastor or pastoral teaching team is planning to engage the congregation in roughly six weeks of campaign messages, it could look something like this:

Week 1	**Vision for the Future** A message about who we are and where we are headed
Week 2	**How God Is at Work Now** A message celebrating the current ministry and mission of the church
Week 3	**The Connection between Heart and Money** A basic teaching on how Jesus views money potentially threatening our allegiance to God
Week 4	**God Is the Ultimate Giver** A message on how one of the foundational theologies of our faith is rooted in God the Father's act of grace and giving in the death of His Son
Week 5	**How Investment Turns into Returns**

	Explain that while returns are not financial, they are deeply impactful. Relate the capital project to its ability to further ministry.
Week 6	**What Commitment Means for God's People** A teaching on how covenantal relationships are the way God and God's people show faithfulness to what is truly important

In each of these worship services, as mentioned in chapter 9 on developing discipleship themes and practices, there can be both information given about the campaign and its projects as well as inspiration via testimonies or teaching in addition to the pastor.

Participant

The senior pastor will have a participatory role in the campaign that is both professional (the campaign process) and personal (their own giving).

Campaign Process

Because pastors are the most visible and vocal person in the articulation of clear vision, they need to be ready for extra meetings and events during the public phase of the campaign.

Whether it is a one-on-one meeting with a major donor household over dinner or lunch, a small group, or a large event the church is conducting, their voice is vital to the success of the campaign.

As much as the volunteers (and staff) will bear the brunt of campaign execution to alleviate the pastor, there is no one that can do what the pastor is called to do in these circumstances.

NOTE: Early in the calendar development process of campaign preparation, the pastor will want to understand the implications on schedule and be realistic about margin and rest during this time.

Preaching responsibilities often continue but every other nonessential duty needs to be "cleared" or delegated so that the campaign does not lead to burnout. It can be really enjoyable for a pastor to visit with people in a unique way as long as there are times of rejuvenation built in as well.

Personal Giving

One of the key features of effective campaigns is that the leaders of the church are not asking the congregation to do something that they are not willing to do themselves. One of the most important roles the pastor can play is as a member of the body, as he or she chooses to engage the prayers and decisions regarding financial sacrifice that everyone is being asked to exercise.

> Transformation begins with you. You cannot ask others to go where you have not gone yourself, in both internal values and external actions.

I have seen great effectiveness come from the pastor being very specific about the level of the gift his household is choosing to commit. Though this is not required or comfortable for some churches, the more specific the modeling of generosity can be, the better.

If the church chooses to utilize a "Lead Gifts" process, then the pastor (and the staff) should be among the families going ahead of the congregation with an early pledge.

Questions to Consider

Have we considered the impact on the senior pastor and are we willing to rearrange his priorities and responsibilities to allow for the campaign demands?

What will be the most difficult part about this temporary re-prioritization?

List some of the positive outcomes the pastor may experience during this time period:

Are there others that have credibility and authority at our church that could shoulder the weight of either the campaign work or the regular work of the pastor? Who are they?

Chapter Seven

Three Segments of Givers

Givers give.

It is a mantra that will help considerably in prioritizing your time and effort.

I have regularly been asked over the last two decades about people who are not currently giving and whether or not the campaign will inspire them to start. This question comes from a place of excitement and optimism. "There are a few hundred families that don't give anything yet—imagine if they decided to give because of the campaign?!"

The reality of giving in the church is that, with few exceptions, every church is funded by about 60 percent of the people that attend—meaning, it has up to 40 percent of its people who will not make a gift that can be recorded and attributed to them. In a capital campaign, only those who have already shown an inclination to regularly support the church financially will consider going "above and beyond" their financial support for a campaign.

Years ago, Pat Graham, former President of Cargill Associates, taught me the rule of 60/60. The rule was that 60 percent of people in any church give a gift that can be attributed to them, and 60 percent of that subset of people will give to a capital project. There certainly have been variations on this theme, but this statistic (or axiom) is closer to the truth than I want it to be. I encourage church leaders to pray for 100 percent participation but plan for a financial response that seems to fit the pattern of most churches.

There is something unique, as well, about the level of giving a person or couple is practicing. There is a different kind of conversation that can be had with various segments or tiers of the giving population of a church.

NOTE: For this conversation, I tend to use the word "households" to represent a person or family from which giving comes. Others may use "giving units" or a different term. Couples (with rare exceptions) tend to give as a family unit.

Very simply, there needs to be a slightly if not substantially different approach to three groups:

Givers
Top 20 Percent of Givers
Top 1 Percent of Givers

Givers

These are the people of the church that have a registered gift in the contribution system. In other words, if people only give cash, we have no record of that unless an envelope system is used. If they use an envelope, then their gift is considered a "recorded gift." This number is often readily known or understood by church leadership. This group makes up everyone who is in the church database system with a recorded gift; one-time givers, people that don't attend a church but gave at one point, consistent givers, large givers, small givers, etc.

Disclaimer: For the sake of practicality, I will not make the caveat every time that the size of the gift is not more or less worthy or spiritual. Please understand that a relatively "small" gift may be enormously faithful and "spiritually big" in the eyes of God. Consider the impoverished widow who gave two copper coins that Jesus described as more generous than all the other givers. While we don't have God's eyes, we do attempt to be faithful and strategic and use an admittedly imperfect grid. There are few alternatives.

This is a critical data point that consultants start with to get a sense for the overall potential of a campaign. Often, the giving level and number of households participating can give clues (not exact indicators) of the amount of potential pledges for the capital campaign. Again, this is the 60/60 rule.

There is a statistical probability that 60 percent of these households will register a pledge. For the math wizards that are already ahead of me, 60 percent of 60 percent is 36 percent. So, you can count on 36 percent of the population of a church participating in a capital campaign.

This overall number represents a church's **POTENTIAL.**

Top 20 Percent of Givers

Some could argue that the 80/20 (Pareto) principle applies to substantive giving in the context of the church. I would not disagree. At the risk of confusion, I tend to classify this group of people into either the top 10 or 20 percent of households depending on church size.

Interestingly, the Pareto principle is not merely an urban myth without some level of backing. This principle states that "for many events, roughly 80 percent of the effects come from 20 percent of the causes."

Consider the following:

- Roughly 80 percent of the world's wealth is held by roughly 20 percent of the people
- In the last few decades, 20 percent of Americans paid 80 percent of the federal taxes
- 80 percent of crimes are committed by about 20 percent of the people[13]

One study, cited by Donor Search, indicates that 88 percent of capital campaign gifts come from 12 percent of the givers. Whether this study remains completely accurate by the time you read this paragraph is not the point. The point is that a minority of the people will make a majority of the impact. Most are not surprised at this since it applies to other areas of church life as well.

Each church can have their financial records keeper do a quick study on the source of a majority of the giving. There is usually a recognizable "drop off " point in the giving that can be used as a way to categorize. Again, this is an imperfect process and takes the spiritual dynamic of giving out of the equation, but stick with me. We need to do a little math as a planning tool; then we will circle back to the spiritual stuff.

I was taught to study congregational giving behavior by using questions like: What percentage of givers account for 80 percent of the dollars given?

This quick inquiry will give the church a sense for the best "pool" of candidates for over-and-above giving. These households tend to be the ones that pay attention, have emotional ownership of the church's future, and will likely take an invitation to participate in a capital campaign seriously. This is the core—the group of people that make a massive difference in the future of the church in all categories including the giving part of church life.

If we are establishing this tier at a church of less than five hundred in attendance, I would group the top 20 percent of giving households. At a larger church, I may tend to cluster the top 10 percent so that it is a manageable "group" with whom to interact.

This is a representation of the church's high potential group.

Top 1 Percent of Givers

To each church, God seems to supply some households that are very wealthy. My experience has been limited to modern Christians in America, so this may not be true everywhere, but there is a small segment of members at even small churches that have capacity that is so high most of us would not even know how to relate.

For specific instructions and advice on dealing with major donors, be sure to study chapter 10. The point of bringing this up here is that it represents an important part of the three tiers of giving.

The best practice in terms of capital campaigns is that this group, whether it be two families or twenty, can engage in a different kind of discussion than most of the congregation.

These are people that have the ability to make a lead gift or top gift, or at least make a significant impact on the overall need. They are accustomed to having people from other organizations speak with them in a direct but kind manner that is often missing in the church. Not considering how God could use someone like this would be a significant missed opportunity.

What if part of the reason God gave them enormous resources or the ability to accumulate wealth was because He wanted to use it for His purposes in some way? These are precious people that are often alone in their thoughts and decisions about their stewardship and usually would welcome a conversation with one of their pastors about how to leverage what God has given them for greater impact.

This is a representation of the church's **high capacity group**.

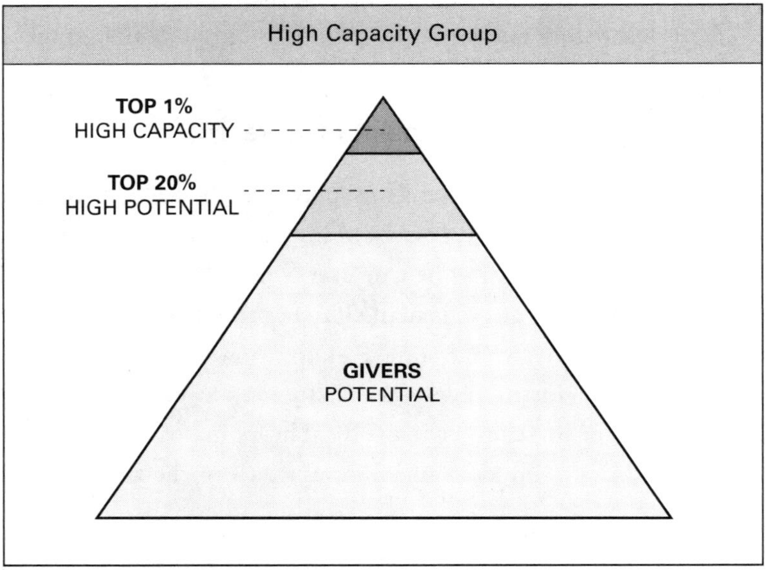

Figure 7.1

Questions to Consider

Is there anything about our church culture, theology, or philosophy that would make segmented giving strategies difficult?

How many total giving households are there at the church?

What will givers get to hear, learn, or experience during the campaign? Is this different than what attenders hear through the course of the initiative? Are there special meetings or mailings? Anything else uniquely planned for this group?

How many households are in the top 20 percent of the above number?

(For example, if you have 1,000 giving units, then 100 households are the top 10 percent irrespective of dollar amount.)

What will the top 10 percent of givers get to hear, learn, or experience during the campaign? Is this different than others? Are there special meetings or mailings? Anything else uniquely planned for this group?

How many are in the top 1 percent of the total giving households? (Some churches may want to just decide on a number of families—like ten—instead of a percentage of givers.)

How do we want to engage this small number of families individually? Do we have a strategy for gracefully challenging these friends for lead gifts or matching gifts? (See chapter 10 "Considerations for Major Donors.")

Chapter Eight

Three Giving Constructs

When it comes to coaching a senior leadership team, I always try to illustrate the way that the dollars and cents actually move, flow, and fund the church.

We call these pictures or sketches on a white board "constructs." They are the ways that we can quickly help leaders visualize possibilities and realities. Some graphics are used for planning and leadership conversations "in house." Other constructs can be helpful with the campaign communication as people are trying to find their place in the overall equation.

We will discuss the following three constructs:

Inverted Triangles

Giving Chart

Levels of Giving

Inverted Triangles

This simple diagram allows for an understanding of the importance of segmenting and nurturing the top-end of the giving list. Quite frankly, when church leaders see this, they know it is true. And then they realize that we would do best to think about specific ways we can engage with people at all levels. This is an internal document for teaching and strategizing purposes only.

It relates back to the discussion of the givers, the top 20 percent and the top 1 percent from chapter 7.

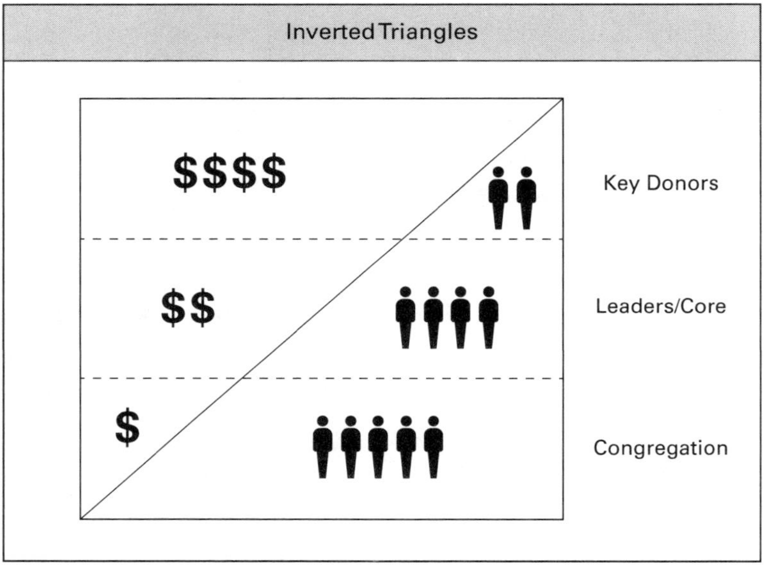

Figure 8.1

Another way of looking at the Inverted Triangles . . .

It is helpful to diagnose the breakdown of giving in your congregation. Even at a cursory level, it is wise to understand how many (or who) may be in the top part of the giving distribution. Would you say there are five families or fifty? What level of inclination to give do we presume these households have for our project? (See chapter 10 for more specifics on this.)

When church leaders do a very simple "back of the napkin" breakdown of how giving happens, it usually reveals some questions we need to ask ourselves about our approach to meetings and methodology during the campaign and after. If you were filling this chart out quickly, what would you estimate? Ask your financial records keeper to help provide an accurate top-level understanding of this as you plan and proceed.

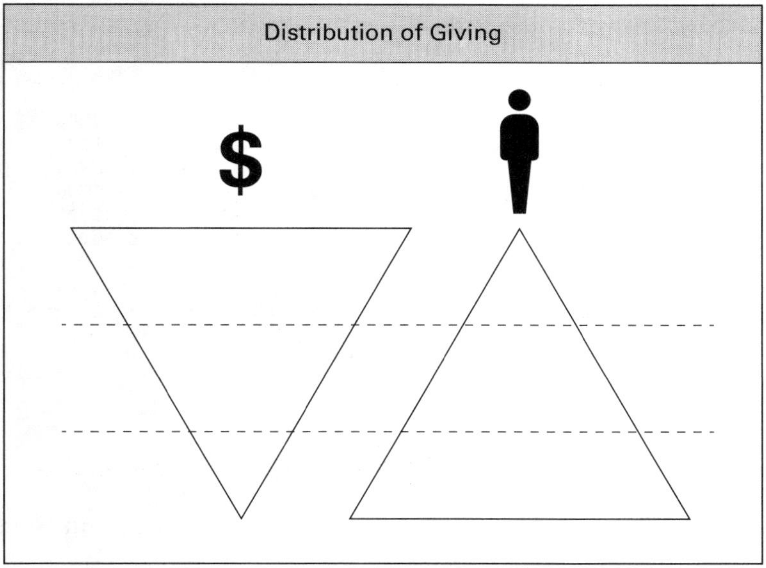

Figure 8.2

Giving Chart

The Giving Chart helps by doing the math for the donor. It allows for everyone to see that seemingly small gifts are not so small and are necessary to make the campaign successful. This matrix answers the question so many have: How could my $30 each week make a difference? Won't the rich people foot the bill for this campaign?

When the chart shows that $30 per week is an almost $5,000 gift to the church, it substantiates the idea that both financially and spiritually we want everyone involved at whatever level God enables them to participate.

Giving Chart			
GIVEN WEEKLY	GIVEN MONTHLY	GIVEN ANNUALLY	3-YEAR TOTAL
$2,000	$8,666.00	$104,000	$312,000
$1,000	$4,333.33	$ 52,000	$156,000
$ 500	$2,166.67	$ 26,000	$ 78,000
$ 300	$1,300.00	$ 15,600	$ 46,800
$ 200	$ 866.67	$ 10,400	$ 31,200
$ 150	$ 650.00	$ 7,800	$ 23,400
$ 100	$ 433.33	$ 5,200	$ 15,600
$ 75	$ 325.00	$ 3,900	$ 11,700
$ 60	$ 260.00	$ 3,120	$ 9,360
$ 50	$ 216.67	$ 2,600	$ 7,800
$ 40	$ 173.33	$ 2,080	$ 6,240
$ 30	$ 130.00	$ 1,560	$ 4,680

Figure 8.3

Levels of Giving

There are a number of ways this "pyramid" can be designed and presented. The bottom line is that this kind of graphic communicates a few important concepts:

1. It shows that the church can achieve its goal—it is not silly or dreamy to think about the target we are setting in front of people.
2. It shows that lead or top givers are needed as well as those in the middle and those with

seemingly small gifts. We cannot achieve this without each other.

3. The graphic also allows major donors to start thinking and praying about a level of gift that is needed. They need to ask and answer the question, "What does my church need me to do?" If the top giving levels are in the hundreds of thousands, they have what they need to start thinking and praying.

As a side note, I used to think that this was too "secular" and the church should not need to stoop to such unholy methodologies—until I realized that God gives amazing grace and intellect to people in other areas that we use all the time—medicine, law, arts, and more. Why not at least consider what God has allowed these experts to learn? We may choose to modify it or even not use it, but to ignore it or look down on it seems irrational.

From the team at doublethedonation.com we find a helpful discussion starter for a Levels of Giving matrix:

Begin with your fundraising goal as your starting point. For simplicity's sake, let's assume you need to raise $500,000.

Next, you'll need to estimate the largest gift you'll be able to secure. Depending on your organization, this will likely be between 15 percent and 30 percent of your fundraising goal. Let's call it 20 percent, or $100,000 in this example.

Then, calculate the next highest gift amounts. The easiest way to do this is by halving each consecutive gift level.

So, in our example, the giving levels would be:

- $50,000
- $25,000
- $12,500
- $6,250

Then, assign the number of donations you'll need for each giving level to reach your goal. In this example, we'll need:

- 1 donation of $100,000
- 2 donations of $50,000
- 4 donations of $25,000
- 8 donations of $12,500
- 16 donations of $6,250

The idea is to bring in a few large donations and many smaller ones. There are a number of ways to come up with a model like this. When I was originally coached to do this, the general notion was that one household is likely capable of 10 percent or more of the total.

Then, two households would "cover" the next 10 percent, then four households for another 10 percent and then after our top 10 percent of giving families the gift sizes tend to be a few thousand dollars each for their three-year total pledge amount. The following model is simply a way to help this church of 700 giving households determine a way forward in an effort to raise $4M. (See Figure 8.4.)

This is not intended to be exact in terms of the calculation—the top line is intentionally left open so that someone is not limited to only give the top amount listed. And the bottom of this chart is indicating that all gift levels (whether they are as high as the ones listed or not) are significant to the success of the campaign.

Levels of Giving to Produce $4,000,000		
Number of Gifts	Gifts At	Amount
——	Gifts At	——
1	Gift At	$ 400,000
2	Gifts At	$ 200,000
4	Gifts At	$ 100,000
6	Gifts At	$ 75,000
10	Gifts At	$ 50,000
20	Gifts At	$ 25,000
40	Gifts At	$ 10,000
60	Gifts At	$ 6,000
75	Gifts At	$ 4,500
——	Gifts At	——

Figure 8.4

Chapter Nine

Three Elements of Discipleship

In the context of the church, discussions about giving and generosity are ultimately a matter of discipleship. A disciple is one who believes in Jesus and lives according to His teaching. The underlying belief is that the way someone handles their finances cannot be separated from their spiritual health as a disciple.

It is no small observation that Jesus regularly mentioned money and possessions in His teaching. Since He did not need to fundraise, He must have known that spiritual wholeness has something to do with belief and behavior concerning finances.

The openhandedness that comes from a life of faith is directly tied to spiritual formation and faith maturity. This is one of the characteristics of a church capital campaign that is distinct from other fundraising efforts. The engagement with the congregation needs to be about finances, yes, but also much more. It is an opportunity for members of the church to have a "checkup" of sorts—not about their physical health, but about their management of the resources that God has entrusted to them.

The reality is, the way we handle our money reveals the posture of our hearts. A church capital campaign, then, will reveal to people the state of their hearts in regards to their relationship with Jesus.

Campaigns are great spiritual diagnostic tools for our church—both gauging and challenging the current spiritual condition of our people. Beyond procuring finances, there truly is an opportunity to see people grow in the sincerity with which they follow Jesus.

For the campaign to be discipleship-oriented, it should contain elements like the following:

Prayer

Teaching

Self-Reflection

Prayer

A campaign is a time of importance in the spiritual life of any person who is taking their church and its future seriously. As much as we would like to believe that this posture is how people make decisions regularly, some may choose to make a financial decision without exercising spiritual muscles like prayer. This is a missed opportunity to practice the spiritual disciplines of prayer, sacrifice, exhibiting faith, and more. Answering the following question could be a fruitful exercise for a church leadership team: *What about the traditional spiritual disciplines (prayer, fasting, solitude, etc.) apply to developing a heart of generosity?*

One of the amazing features I have seen at the heart of the capital campaign process is the idea that people are praying audacious and abnormal prayers. We rarely have opportunities in our Christian journey where we say words to God like, "Lord, I am thinking about pledging $10,000 to our church, but I need You to affirm that or change my mind." There is an added element for married people. The most difficult conversations to have in most marriages (statistics tell us) are about money. Add to this already difficult conversation that a couple is considering additional giving to their church. This may lead to a conversation that has been avoided or neglected in a marriage. With proper guidance, we have seen couples go to a new level in both their generosity and the intimacy of their marriage. It requires a spiritual conversation, asking questions like, "What is our life, family, and marriage all about? What are our true priorities? Should we be adjusting something to reflect our values?"

Sean Mitchell, from Generosity Development, highlights the importance of prayer as well as basic steps to implement a prayer emphasis during the course of the campaign:

1. Church leaders, pastors, and elders, will need to lead the way and practice what it is hoped others will practice. This group will need to gather and collectively create a group prayer plan. When will you collectively pray? For how long? What will you use as a guide for your prayer?
2. During the campaign, urge your congregation to pray. Do it not once, but repeatedly. How can you use the platform of the campaign to teach them to pray? How can you remind them that prayer is for all seasons of life and needs to be a core priority of our discipleship?
3. Those who write extensively on prayer and lead prayer retreats often encourage praying people to practice "watching." The encouragement

> is to keep a journal and track what you are "asking" God for in prayer, the cares you are referencing, and the words and messages you hear in your prayerful silence. After months of journaling, the praying will look back (watch) for the ways God may have answered certain prayers. I would encourage church leaders to practice "watching" and encourage congregants to do so as well.[14]

One accessible yet dangerous prayer that can easily and beautifully infiltrate a congregation is the one that asks, "God, what would You have me give or give up to invest in Your work through my church?"

One of the teams that many churches will choose to utilize during a capital campaign is a prayer team (mentioned in chapter 5). The prayer team may already exist at your church. If not, you can create one to allow the congregation to experience:

- A prayer meeting
- A prayer emphasis
- A prayer devotional
- A prayer walk

Teaching

Many churches are underdeveloped in the category of teaching about giving and generosity. The campaign provides a prime opportunity to develop this area. Only 15 percent of pastors say they have been equipped by their denomination or seminary to teach biblical financial principles.[15] Add to the lack of training the fact that people (including pastors) are reticent to talk about money in almost any setting. This is a recipe for virtual silence about a crucially important topic in the life of a Christian.

I challenge churches everywhere I go by asserting that it is malpractice for church leaders to ignore teaching about money.

Money woes are the number one reason for stress in marriage, the primary reason people are anxious or worried, the cause for broken sibling relationships, and often the story behind why once best friends are now hated enemies. So many people come limping into our churches because of career, financial, and relational angst, and then most churches are silent about how God's view of money can free us from being trapped and stressed.

Rick Warren passionately asserts that one of the single most important tasks of leadership is teaching people how to give.

> In reality, very few things come close to the importance of this task, for one of God's purposes for our lives is that we become like Jesus. The only way we are ever going to become like Jesus is if we learn to give radically: generously, without restraint, liberally, over-the-top giving.
>
> God so loved the world that He gave. God wants me to become like Him, not as a "god" but as godly. Therefore, one of the most important lessons in life, both for me personally and in my leadership and discipleship of others, is to learn how to become incredibly, outrageously generous.[16]

It is fascinating to me that one of the primary catalysts in being made like Jesus is my ability to practice countercultural living and giving. At this point, it is even "counter" to most church people, who give minimally (2.5% of income) and act and behave just like non-churched people.

David Kinnaman of the Barna Group takes this discussion about teaching to an even more intense level in *The Generosity Gap*:

> So often we focus our efforts on cultivating generous habits rather than on making generous disciples. Of course, the former is a vitally significant part of accomplishing the latter; people are less likely to grow spiritually without concrete disciplines like practicing generosity. But the practices themselves are not the point. The point is who we become under the influence of our habits.[17]
>
> When we attend to the condition of our minds, hearts and souls, the limits of our generosity are stretched and our giving capabilities strengthened.[18]

Self-Reflection

One of the key features of creating a spiritual formation audit as an element of a capital campaign is to ask people to think through their own personal beliefs about giving. More specifically, they can look in the mirror to see if what they believe is played out in their actual behavior. They may discovery it is time for a re-start.

If all of the adults in the congregation do a personal "checkup" of the condition of their generosity, it could be very powerful, both spiritually and financially. We could encourage people to ask themselves:

- What are the characteristics of generous people?

- How would I rate myself according to those characteristics?
- What motivates me to be generous?
- How does my faith drive my desire to live with open hands?
- Does my giving reflect the priorities I claim to hold?
- Is there a way I need to rethink my giving intensity or amount?

I believe everyone has a money wiring. Our family of origin, our good and bad experiences, our belief in God, and probably a few more things inform our money temperament. Ultimately, the people that have a good handle on money, whether they are rich or poor, are some of the most attractive people to be around. It requires a level of spiritual health that few of us possess.

I have had the privilege of working with one of the most open-handed and generous people I have ever met. He is the founding pastor of the church we have raised our children in and into which my wife and I have invested a significant portion of our lives, both on and off the church staff.

What attracts a person at first to Steve Andrews is his winsome and unexpectedly normal demeanor. He is the pastor of a megachurch with multiple satellites and church plants and a global ministry. His impact has likely touched tens of thousands of people.

He lives in a normal house, drives a normal car, and wears hand-me-down shirts (much to the chagrin of his family and friends). He has given away much of his money to the various capital campaigns our church has had (five of them!) and has supported his children, grandchildren, and extended family for decades. How does this kind of a life happen?

Steve wrote about growing up in the house of his parents, Dr. Chubby and Margie Andrews in Memphis in the '50s and '60s. He has vivid memories of his parents opening their home and giving away their lives for other people as they were motivated by God's goodness to them. He told me they gave away their food, cars, and living space—he remembers as a boy that his parents hosted Bible studies that would bring 100 people to the house at a time. He writes in his personal memoir:

> Who are the happiest and most loving people you know? My guess is that your mind instantly goes to generous people! I have been surrounded by people my whole life who gave away huge portions of their income, huge portions of their free time, huge portions of their relational energy. And without fail they are the healthiest, most joyful people I know! Generous people believe in the goodness and faithfulness of God. They are willing to risk because they know Jesus cares about every detail of their lives. And I know this, when I keep a death grip on my stuff and my money and my time that's when I am most miserable and most dangerous to others.[19]

Author and pastor Henri Nouwen wrote that the work of the church in this category is actually a "call to conversion."[20] He explains that to be converted in this way means to experience a deep shift in how we see and think and act. It is a shift of attention in which we allow ourselves to "not be conformed to this age, but be transformed by the renewing of your mind" (Rom. 12:2).

One of the classic capital campaign passages many will refer to is what was happening during David's reign and the response of the leaders and people to the ancient campaign efforts of the Israelites. Here we read a stunning example of the humility with which we can approach “extra” giving: “But who am I, and who are my people, that we should be able to give as generously as this? For everything comes from you, and we have given you only what comes from your hand” (1 Chron. 29:14).

Again, it should be said that prayer, teaching, and self-reflection does not mean that money or talk of funding a church dream is a bad or “lower” thing. But the campaign can be about both spiritual and financial success. This is the next level.

I believe churches can run effective capital campaigns without an expressed intent to deepen the spiritual commitments of the congregation. I have helped run such campaigns. I also believe that church leadership needs to have a serious dialogue about what is implied by these parallel concepts of both devotion and generosity.

Please consider and discuss the following comparison and, more importantly, what this may imply for how your campaign is designed.

Campaign Comparisons	
Fundraising-Only Campaign	**Discipleship-Based Campaign**
Funding Projects	Practicing Generosity
Personal Financial Audit	Personal Spiritual Audit
Financial Consideration	Prayerful Consideration
Thermometer of Giving	Thermostat of Spiritual Condition
Shift in Spending	Shift in Perspective
Budgeting Disciplines	Spiritual Disciplines
Success is Financial Increase	Success is Faith Increase
Giving Dependent on Income	Giving Dependent on Provision
Money Comes From Me	Money Comes From God
Generous Habits	Generous Disciples

Figure 9.1

Questions to Consider

Do we have the intention to make a capital campaign as much about deep self-reflection of disciples as we do about hitting financial targets?

List the features of the campaign that are about the financial aspect of the campaign:

1. ____________________

2. ____________________

3. ____________________

4. ____________________

List the features of the campaign that lean toward the spiritual development of the members of the congregation:

1. ____________________

2. ____________________

3. ____________________

4. ____________________

Chapter Ten

Three Considerations for Major Donors

Calling someone a major donor in the context of the church may sound indelicate to some. It is certainly a title that comes from the philanthropic community outside the church. Call them what you will—high-net-worth families, people with means—God has given some in the church the gift of financial means that allow them to be a part of a resource ministry in an extraordinary way, particularly if they are inclined to help financially or have the spiritual gift of giving.

They are technically not major donors until they make a major donation of some kind. And this is a subjective term. Some are already acting as major donors and others have potential to contribute at a high level. The easiest way to describe these families is that they are at the top of your general giving list and have the capability to make a significant contribution over-and-above giving.

The fact is: Some households can (and often will) give 10 percent or more of the total amount needed.[21]

Ben Witherington writes about the apostle Paul in his commentary on Philippians: "There is also considerable evidence that Paul's missionary strategy involved not only an urban focus but also a practical focus on converting high status persons who could be sponsors for a fledgling Christian community, including housing it."[22]

Nurturing high-net-worth individuals and families is an area of study and expertise unto itself. Entire books have been written about this for fund development officers outside the church. To most pastors, this activity seems foreign—like something that happens at universities and museums, but not in the parish. Many ministry leaders will "opt out" of even trying to engage with these families. But a simple three-category approach to thinking about these individuals or couples may help increase confidence in giving it a try in the world of the church. It is really all about an intentional conversation.

Consider these elements of an engagement:

Right Person Asking
Right Person Being Asked
Right Amount and Timing

Right Person Asking

Very simply, this is almost always the senior pastor. There are a few very large churches that may have a group of leaders that can serve in this role, particularly because there would be too many meetings for the senior pastor to handle in terms of time commitment. Either way, the right person is the one who has relationship, trust, and credibility with the family being asked.

Once the plan is made, personal and face-to-face meetings need to be arranged. The rule of thumb is that larger gifts are discussed in smaller settings. Author and consultant Kim Klein explains the considerable difference in effectiveness when comparing face-to-face conversation with almost every other way to ask or inquire in the following chart.[23]

Ladder of Effectiveness

STRATEGY	RESPONSE RATE
Personal Face-to-Face Ask	50%
Personal Phone Call	25%
Personal Letter	10–15%
Direct Mail (Acquisition)	1%
On-line	varies
Special Events	varies

If the right person is asking the right person at the right time for the right amount, the chances of success are considerably higher.

As mentioned, the right person to ask is often the senior pastor. However, we have found that there is a stigma among many ministers regarding their interaction with wealthy people.

Now, where there have been abuses, pastors and church leaders deserve the bad reputation. But most church leaders I have interacted with have sky-high integrity, yet have been scared away from such conversations for reasons that are not fully sound. Often what has been cited to them (or they have taught others) is that approaching a wealthy person in a generosity conversation or "because they have wealth" is a way of giving preferential treatment to the rich that is spoken against in Scripture.

> My brothers and sisters, do not show favoritism as you hold on to the faith in our glorious Lord Jesus Christ. For if someone comes into your meeting wearing a gold ring and dressed in fine clothes, and

> a poor person dressed in filthy clothes also comes in, if you look with favor on the one wearing fine clothes and say, "Sit here in a good place," and yet you say to the poor person, "Stand over there," or "Sit here on the floor by my footstool," haven't you made distinctions among yourselves and become judges with evil thoughts?
>
> Listen, my dear brothers and sisters: Didn't God choose the poor in this world to be rich in faith and heirs of the kingdom that he promised to those who love him? Yet you have dishonored the poor. Don't the rich oppress you and drag you into court? Don't they blaspheme the good name that was invoked over you? (James 2:1–7)

Auxano colleague Dr. Clint Grider cautions that leaders need to be careful in how they apply this passage: "Some pastors, with best of intentions, avoid interacting with large givers or avoid engaging with them directly on matters of generosity, thinking that shepherding people with means is synonymous with 'showing them favor.' Nothing could be further from the truth . . . A passage about an abuse in the first-century church on access to worship gatherings has somehow become a prohibition against intentional pastoral conversations with a guy who drives a BMW."[24]

The result is neglect of people who have significant responsibility to steward resources in a biblical way. God has placed a need in people to do something bigger than themselves, and those with means are seeking how to faithfully and wisely navigate the needs they see and the priorities God has instilled in their hearts. Wealth does not disqualify people from the need for spiritual guidance or intentional discipleship. Church leaders need to build purposeful systems to deepen these conversations in creative, ongoing ways.

Here's how Pat Mclaughlin of the Timothy Group recommends we engage major donors:

- Call to make an appointment. Don't ask for their gift over the phone. Don't send a letter in the mail. And certainly don't just make asks from the pulpit. Direct mail has a 1 to 5 percent response rate, a phone call is 30 percent. A personal ask has a 75 percent success rate.
- Set up a time when both spouses can be present. Find a time that is convenient for them.
- No surprises. Let them know that you are coming to talk about the project, who is coming with you, and how long you will stay.
- They will invite you into the living room to sit on their soft couches, but ask if you can sit at the kitchen or dining room table, instead.
- Tell them about the need, it's importance, and your plan for using the money.
- Show that you value their time by presenting the information about the giving opportunity in 30 minutes.
- Be friendly, polite, and trust them to make the right decision with their money. Ask yourself how you would like to be asked for a gift, and do that.
- After the presentation is done, you can stay if they invite you. Otherwise, thank them for their time, and confirm when you'll follow up with them.
- Follow up with them at the agreed time to hear their commitment decision.[25]

It is fascinating to sit down with Clint Grider, a key member of the Auxano Resourcing Division. He has been part of leadership teams that have raised well over a billion dollars in academic, ministry, and other not-for-profit settings. He brings that experience to the conversation.

Grider often discusses the importance of constantly taking the time to nurture trusting relationships. To achieve this, systems must be in place to engage a variety of natural partners in the dialogue over time.

In church settings, the lead pastor often plays a key role in meeting with high capacity givers, but an effective culture of generosity goes beyond that. A relationship-based progression of conversations with different people, and involvement in purposeful events, forums, and other opportunities may be the most stimulating, appropriate ways to deepen someone's ownership and passion in what God is doing.

Natural Partner: This is someone with whom a financial contributor has already built a trust relationship. "Pastor Jim is willing to meet with the Willis Family, but they already have a natural partner in Andy."

Right Person Being Asked

We have an imperfect but helpful tool when it comes to deciding who is a possible lead giver or major donor. The church database can provide a list of the top giving families to help start this discussion. I have noticed an interesting phenomenon occurs at many churches when pastors recognize that seemingly wealthy individuals are not in the top giving list. I am frequently asked by pastors about families in their congregation that they know have significant financial means, but have not contributed yet—or have not contributed to the level of what we perceive of their capability.

The pastor will say, "But he's the CEO of ____________" or "They have a multi-million-dollar family business" or "I've seen their house and the cars they drive." All of these observations represent the pastor living in faith and optimism about the possibility of a large contribution—which is the way we want our pastors to live!

They dream this way whether they admit it or not: *Imagine if they gave even a portion of what God has given them?*

I am a pastor and I love this line of optimistic thinking. At the same time, I refer to these wishful dreams as whale hunting expeditions.

Whale hunting is when you are looking for a major gift from a person who has not been showing big-giver generosity yet, at least not to the church.

I remember as a kid, fishing with my Pop Pop Paterson off the shores of New Jersey. With a line in the water, I would daydream of pulling in "the big one." Ironically, there was a money pool established before our charter boat would go out in the Atlantic—the biggest fish won the big money at the end of the day. Let's just say my fishing didn't land me the big money any better than my whale hunting as a pastor and fundraiser.

I encourage pastors to have multiple conversations with people of means, but make sure a majority of them are with people who have already shown faithfulness in their giving to the church. This is time well spent. Whale hunting is not crazy; it just isn't very fruitful.

The pastor or senior leaders of the church may need some assistance in developing a few lists that can be used to coach the pastor on how to spend his or her time. An organization like www.mortarstone.com analyzes information about members of our churches that is available and accessible to direct church leaders on where best to spend their time. It takes a bit of the guesswork out of knowing how to disciple individual givers (based on data about their giving practices and behavior).

Let's take a look at a couple more useful terms we can consider as we develop these lists of potential givers:

A *suspect* is a person in the congregation or on the periphery of the church that you think has means, and you suspect that under the right conditions would make a major gift to your church.

A *prospect* is a person or family in the congregation or on the periphery of the church that has already shown with above-average giving behavior that they are not only capable but inclined to give.

Right Amount and Timing

Knowing the right amount to ask a high capacity giver is a foreign concept to most ministry professionals, and for good reason. There should be a level of discretion, and these conversations shouldn't be indelicate, presumptuous, or frequent.

One of the reasons I recommend a regular and constant pastoral relationship with high-net-worth families from a practical standpoint is that there should be a handful of "no ask" meetings before there is ever one with a major request. Pastors often don't have time to do this or make up for lost ground in the heat of a campaign, but it can and should be a practice moving forward.

When these "ask" meetings do happen, research and experience show that major donors are pleased with the directness of a specific ask, whether they choose to give the requested amount or give a greater or lesser amount.

In his book *Ask for a Fish*, author Ron Hass interviews a business owner and generous giver by the name of Jim DeVries. DeVries goes into detail about being the person on the "receiving end" of asks by ministries and churches.

When discussing the idea of asking for a specific amount, he reveals the following:

> I am never offended when people suggest a gift amount. It lets me know what they have in mind. I might or might not give that amount, but I like knowing what they are thinking. Sometimes I give more than they ask. Recently, someone shared a giving opportunity with me but never asked for money. That's fine, but in reality, she was looking for a gift . . . instead, she left a brochure and I put it on my desk. The next week another ministry came and presented their need, then another, and then another. Her brochure quickly got buried in the bottom of my pile. The moral of the story is that it's okay to ask. I appreciate it when people ask for what they want.[26]

As we are discussing the idea of the "right amount," it is not meant to imply that there is a right amount or a wrong amount. The point is that we can only make a prayerful and educated guess or estimate as to what we think the donor family may be able to contribute. If it is not an amount that is appropriate for that household, it does not mean that they will be discouraged or angry. What it means is that they will need to adjust your expectations by responding with the reality of their situation and means.

Years ago, I had the honor of spending some time with Paul Edwards, who is a leading voice in donor development—at that time he was investing most of his energy on behalf of Wycliffe Bible Translators. There are things he said in those few days that still stick with me because they were so helpful. He also left behind (very generously) pages of notes and files for my use. In one of those files, he explained how he discusses major gift targeting in the context of a capital campaign.

There are two things to keep in mind as you read the next few paragraphs highlighting the notes Paul left behind for me. First, as you are aware, times have radically changed. Second, Paul Edwards was raising money for a para-church organization, usually in a five-year collection period. Still, these thoughts from Edwards can be adjusted for your context as well as style of asking. He reminds us that:

1. Liquidity is the key—the funds are needed sooner rather than later.
2. As a general rule, people tithe (or give regularly) from the day-to-day cash flow that comes with income; whereas capital gifts come from assets saved over time such as stocks, real estate holdings, and other non-cash goods.
3. Major gifts are ten or more times the individual's annual gift over a five-year period.

He also provided an "Ask Script" which may be very helpful to pastors and church leaders who do not have this experience:

- Summarize how things are going
- Briefly describe the opportunity
- Make an ask with a specified amount
- Listen in silence
- Respond to questions and objections
- Use four key questions when you get a no:
  - Is it our church?
  - The project?
  - The amount?
  - The timing?
- Summarize next steps

In my experience in church campaigns, it is not far off the mark to ask a household to consider an amount that is five times their annual gift in the form of a three-year pledge (in a two-year pledge, it should be three times their annual gift).

Remember that this is usually out of assets and over multiple years. A three-year campaign, for instance, usually happens in four charitable giving fiscal years, a two-year campaign happens in three giving years and so on.

In this conversation, there is a chance that the family or couple may say, "Pastor, we are honored that you would ask us to give that amount, but we are not in a position to do that right now." This is a totally fair and helpful exchange between a person and their pastor or church leader. First, it shows that they would give if the timing were different, which is encouraging. Second, it indicates that if something changes, there still could be a way to make a significant contribution. A conversation can then ensue about what obstacles need to clear for the couple to give at a substantial level and if there is a creative way to still achieve a gift inside the campaign window.

A Caution to My Fellow Pastors

If you are a pastor reading this, please remember that it is difficult to think about these questions in terms of your own assets. This can sometimes deter you from being bold and allowing God to do His work in the potential donor's mind and heart.

I can relate to this. The campaign I led as senior pastor was at a time of my life when my wife and I were poor as church mice (pardon the exaggeration). Asking someone for a major gift felt like I was a peasant approaching a king (pardon another hyperbole).

As pastors, sometimes we allow our own financial means or our own lack of comfort about this topic to become the main obstacle to God using us to shepherd a major donor.

I encourage you not to think, *I can't ask this couple to consider a $50,000 gift to the church—I can't even fathom that!* The fact is, that family you are asking may be making multiple gifts of that level in one year.

According to the Giving USA website (givingusa.org), this is the breakdown of charitable giving for 2019:

$124.52 billion	Religion
$58.72 billion	Education
$51.54 billion	Human Services
$50.29 billion	Foundations
$40.78 billion	Health
$31.21 billion	Public/Society Benefit
$19.49 billion	Arts/Culture/Humanities
$22.88 billion	International Affairs
$12.70 billion	Environment & Animal organizations

That "religion" is still the primary recipient of charitable giving in America implies that there is an opportunity that may be missed if we are reticent to initiate the conversation. We may just end up missing out on the opportunity to have major donors engage with the church in a new and deeper way. And we may miss a large gift to the campaign.

One frustrated church member in Michigan recently came to a senior leader and said, "You are not asking me for enough!" The woman who said this is high capacity and her life is very busy. She is leading other organizations, is involved with other charitable work, and cannot simply guess what the church needs. And, she explained that other churches and charities are coming to her and are not afraid to ask directly and specifically. In essence, she was challenging the senior leader at her church to help her manage God's resources in the best way to support her church. She was also indicating that he should become comfortable enough to approach her in a natural way as a member of the congregation and a friend of the ministry.

In my years of gaining courage to meet with successful people, I have come to learn that they are often lonely, and the church does not always know what to do with them. I have talked to more than a few "corner office" people who are isolated and are facing spiritual and practical challenges they never have faced before. Their reality is they have more money and stuff to manage than ever, they can't talk to their employees about their personal challenges, everyone is out to get something or gain something from them, and their spouse is exhausted listening to the stress-laden downloads from the office each evening.

Pastors often think, *If I approach them, they will think it is about their money.* The fact is these friends often need spiritual help in navigating their complicated life. They are not more special than other parts of the church body. They should not be either revered or ignored because of their wealth. At the same time, they do have something to provide just like singers, teachers, and others have their unique means of contribution to the church. And to not talk about their ability to support the church financially would be conspicuous in its absence from the conversation. It is their reality. And you are their pastor.

Many pastors understandably have a hard time being direct about this because it is not a financial world in which they live or function. Yet, our high-net-worth families are having these discussions often with other groups soliciting their support.

In ten years of my work with my friend Alex Calder between 2006 and 2016—including two major (over $20M) church capital campaigns under our co-leadership—we developed an unofficial grid for what amount to approach major donors with in regard to their capital gift.

Perhaps this grid, though imperfect and hardly scientific, could be useful to you as you consider your plans:

Major Donor Strategy		
Annual Gift	2-year Pledge Ask	3-year Pledge Ask
$ 5,000	$ 15,000	$ 25,000
$ 10,000	$ 30,000	$ 50,000
$ 15,000	$ 45,000	$ 75,000
$ 20,000	$ 60,000	$100,000
$ 25,000	$ 75,000	$125,000
$ 40,000	$120,000	$200,000
$ 50,000	$150,000	$250,000

Figure 10.1

Prospects, Suspects and Natural Partners		
Prospects	Natural Partners	
________	________	________
________	________	________
________	________	________
Suspects	Natural Partners	
________	________	________
________	________	________
________	________	________

Figure 10.2

Questions to Consider

Does our church leadership have regular interactions with people of wealth to shepherd them and pastor them? Will our theology and practice allow that?

Do we have a sense of permission to segment givers in this way and interact with them in an honest fashion regarding their wealth? Do we have permission to talk about this idea and strategy with our church leaders?

List some Prospects, Suspects, and their Natural Partners as a beginning step to forming a strategy in this category of the campaign:

Chapter Eleven

Three Categories of Content

The content of capital campaign communication needs to be clear and focused. Capital campaign content contains three key elements: a spiritual renewal exercise, congregational change management, and marketing a new idea to a large group of people.

As we have already discussed in the Shaping the Narrative and Case for Support sections, the articulation of where we are headed as a church needs to be crystal clear, vision-based, and anticipatory of people's questions and hesitations about the journey toward making a pledge.

I will often joke that a well-written FAQ and a Pledge Card is all that is needed to have a great campaign. Realistically, a thorough job of communicating involves covering more than that. The following focuses on that content, irrespective of how it is delivered. (Methodology is discussed in the next chapter.) How we choose to format, write, say, or display this information is critical to a successful endeavor.

The three categories of content that should drive the campaign are:

Vision
Project Focus
Giving

Vision

In a stunning fundraising success not long ago, Harvard University added approximately $200 million to its endowment in just one year. Did they need it? Perhaps not. There are plenty of organizations and colleges that could have used that money more than Harvard. So, what made the difference in Harvard's fundraising efforts? They had a crystal-clear vision on top of earned trust and respect.

> There is at least one thing about which we can all agree: Lack of clarity about the direction of the church can hinder the success of a capital campaign.

Popular author and speaker Simon Sinek became nearly a household name because of his concept of answering your "why" before you can get people to buy into your "what." In the case of marketplace advice, he was saying that people are not as interested in your product as they are interested in the story behind it.

In his bestseller, *Start with Why: How Great Leaders Inspire Everyone to Take Action*, Sinek writes that leadership "requires two things: a vision of the world that does not yet exist and the ability to communicate it."[27]

The reason I appreciate the Auxano group so much is that they will not do anything without clarity first. This relentless pursuit of clarity is the key to success for capital campaigns as well.

I was recently with a great church in Florida that asked, "Can we just do the campaign now and work on our clarity later?" As much as I want to accommodate a client, my job is to also serve them well. My response was that, in fact, we really don't have a reason to campaign until we clarify our "why."

There is a lot of talk in the church these days about organizational clarity and structure. Ironically, there is a lack of clarity about what terms like Vision, Mission, Strategy, and Values mean. Here I will define what these terms mean to me and my colleagues at Auxano.

Vision: The picture of our church's future when operating as the best version of itself. If God chose to bless our ideas and dreams, this is what we would look like.

Mission: The specific way we accomplish what God has called us to—primarily to make disciples and operate the way Jesus taught us.

Strategy: The mechanisms we have in place and venues where people can go to undergo the life transformation that is the intention of our mission.

Values: These are the things we hold dear and define the vibe or ethos of our church. These characteristics will be experienced and discovered by anyone who spends time with us. It is what is important to our tribe.

The authors of *The Flight of the Buffalo* write:

> Vision is the beginning point for leading the journey. Vision focuses. Vision inspires. Vision is our alarm clock in the morning, our caffeine in the evening. Vision touches the heart. It becomes the

> criterion against which all behavior is measured. Vision becomes the glasses that tightly focus all of our sights and actions on that which we want to be tomorrow—not what we were yesterday or what we are today. The focus on vision disciplines us to think strategically. The vision is the framework for leading the journey.[28]

So, the question for church leaders is, "Do we have that kind of vision—a vision that inspires and leads the journey?" And if not, how can we get that clear and compelling way to describe the future God has for our church? Why? Because then funding that future makes sense. Without vision, we are just trying to sell a "project" at the church that would be a nice-to-have improvement for our congregation.

Leave it to Henri Nouwen to say something so beautiful about how vision applies to funding in the work of God:

> Fundraising is proclaiming what we believe in such a way that we offer other people an opportunity to participate with us in our vision and mission. Fundraising is precisely the opposite of begging. When we seek to raise funds, we are not saying, "Please could you help us out because lately it's been hard." Rather we are declaring, "We have a vision that is amazing and exciting. We are inviting you to invest yourself through the resources God has given you—your energy, your prayers, and your money—in this work to which God has called us.[29]

Project Focus

The fact is, people are very interested in what we are doing with the money. Yes, they need vision, trust in leadership, and a sense that we are winning (all covered in chapter 2). But, at some point, they want to see the goods. What are we actually building, renovating, expanding, or investing in? When it comes to delivering this content, there are a number of ways to do it. Covered in chapter 12 "Platforms for Communication," there are many channels to "show and tell" the project features.

I recently met with a group in Detroit's Silicon Valley (there is such a thing) where tech companies abound. Many were birthed in this region where I live because of the amount of technology that is connected with the design, innovation, analysis, and marketing of automobiles. My father-in-law worked for GM and retired from Saturn—my wife grew up just down the road.

But this group approached me because they know I help churches with capital campaigns that often involve building and construction projects. They have developed a virtual reality system that will enable members of churches to "walk through" the new church, new sanctuary, new lobby, or whatever the architect has designed—complete with the accurate colors and textures based on the design choices that have been made. Just picture me in a Starbucks wearing those big VR glasses and exclaiming, "Wow! No way! Churches will love this! Wow!!"

Regardless of the level of sophistication, the fact is that part of what you are delivering to people during a campaign is a "kick the tires" way to understand what the church leadership has decided is the next priority.

And most people are visual, so trying to explain something that doesn't exist yet is better with the pictures that are worth a thousand words.

People often want to know:

1. How did we arrive at this design?
2. Did we consider other alternatives?
3. What will it look like?
4. Will the construction disrupt the activities or worship services?
5. When can we start and finish?
6. What if we don't raise enough money?

Take some time to think of other questions people may have in your context:

1. ______________________________

2. ______________________________

3. ______________________________

4. ______________________________

A Word about Debt Campaigns

It should be noted that each year, more than a handful of clients served in the capital campaign world are churches aiming to retire debt. This requires a different set of parameters and communication approach.

Multi-decade stewardship consultant Todd McMichen, a former Auxano Navigator who now leads LifeWay Generosity, offers this helpful grid for understanding church debt:

Four Basic Church Debt Structures

> Church debt can be generally categorized four ways. First, there is the church that has no debt.

These are often established churches with plateaued or declining growth that have not constructed a new facility in many years. Or, they may be young churches that do not own property. There are also a number of vibrant churches that have embraced a no-debt philosophy.

Second is the church with manageable debt. This church is typically stable and able to invest an above-average amount of funds in staffing, ministries, and missions. However, it is not uncommon for this type of church to live in a state of heightened financial awareness until all debt is paid off, even though debt is a small percentage of its annual budget. This church may decline opportunities to develop until all debt is retired or it perceives itself as wisely positioned to seize the future.

Third is the church that has recently completed an expansion project. Its debt total can be up to 30 percent of annual receipts. Finances are tight, but growth is strong and income is growing. This financial stress has been planned for and is temporary. As the church continues to develop and spend wisely, the debt pressure consistently declines.

Finally, there is the church that has a disproportionately high debt amount. It has built too much, declined numerically, or experienced an unexpected turn in the local economy. This can be the result of unwise planning, unrealistic expectations of the future, or a catastrophic event that could not be anticipated.[30]

In the case of the last two groups Todd mentioned, one frequent consideration is to run a debt-reduction capital campaign in the church. There are no pictures to show of construction or renovation, so motivating people because of a new feature to the facility is off the table.

But talk to any church consulting firm, and the suggestions to run a campaign like this center on "freeing funds" for ministry. Most firms will approach this in a very similar way, because it is very straightforward. The campaign content needs to be all about what will happen when we no longer pay X amount in mortgage payments. Consider the following elements in constructing a communications plan on a debt reduction campaign.

History of the Debt: People may not understand that we have debt. They could be new or just uninformed. The point is that we need to back up and give a little history so people know how we arrived at our current situation. Then, we can begin to talk about how to move forward.

Financial Implications of the Debt: The members of the congregation need to know the percentage of the operating budget that is required to handle the debt service. The monthly and annual amounts give people a sense for magnitude and the relative portion of our spending. (Is it 10 percent of our budget? 20 percent?)

Specifics of the Borrowing: Not only is it a good practice to reveal the details of the structure of the loan for full-disclosure, but it can also motivate people. When the congregation realizes how much interest is involved and for how long they will be paying the mortgage, it can make the next step obvious—eliminate the debt as soon as possible.

A Different Set of Pictures: People do want to see what the future looks like and it can be shown by explaining the ministry and mission that can happen or increase when we can reroute resources.

So maybe there are pictures to show after all—pictures of people in community, people on mission, people being discipled and so on.

Giving

Candidly speaking, whenever I hear that a church has a goal to "never do a capital campaign again," I suspect that something is wrong. Perhaps their last campaign was not executed well, there is pain around campaign expectations versus actual results, or the leadership struggles with their own relationship with money.

When leaders struggle with talking about money, it usually means they haven't "put it in its place," so to speak. So, they are reticent to talk about it because it has too much power in their view, resulting in fear instead of faith. Perhaps I am being too critical, but as I indicated in my introduction, I love capital campaigns. Someone who wants to avoid one at all costs is not experiencing the freedom and joy that can be characteristic of a discipleship-based journey.

There is a practical and pastoral reason for running a great campaign. It is widely accepted that there is a large gap between the amount of times Scripture (and particularly Jesus) refer to money and possessions compared to the amount of time we spend on it in our church teaching and discipleship. I believe it is a significant spiritual issue and can be one of the catalysts for explosive spiritual growth in the hearts of our congregation.

Campaigns are greenhouses for growth in discipleship—the right environment, nutrients, and nurture for things to grow. So, campaigns give us a concentrated opportunity to refresh biblical themes of giving. Part of the content to be delivered to the congregation in addition to vision and project specifics is good old-fashioned teaching on biblical generosity.

God Owns Everything: When we think about personal finance, it's easy to make plans about what we're going to do with "our money." But when we think about "our money," it's important to understand what that really means. The money isn't ours in the sense that we own it; it's simply ours in the sense that we're responsible for managing it. The truth is, everything we have belongs to God.

Everyone Is Investing in Something: We've been taught to keep careful watch on our financial portfolios, but God offers us the opportunity to invest in our eternal portfolio. His plan promises eternal yield for His kingdom.

Jesus Invites Us to Live in Abundance: In the Gospel of John, Jesus said He has come to give not just life, but life in abundance through Him. The Bible teaches that an abundant life is a life lived for God.

Giving Grows Our Faith: Giving demonstrates our faith that the God who has provided for us in the past will provide for us in the future. It is the opposite of fear. Fearful people hang on with white-knuckles to anything they can get. Faithful people see everything in life as a gift from God—including their money. Every time we open our hands in generosity, we are saying to God, "This is yours anyway—please use it for your purposes."

More from Rick Warren's sermon "Teaching People to Be Generous":

> I love Proverbs 22:9: "A generous man will himself be blessed." It is such a simple verse, but it is about the joy that comes about in my life when I decide to give. And I love 1 Chronicles 29:9: "The people rejoiced when they had given freely and wholeheartedly to the Lord. David the King also rejoiced greatly."

> Givers don't complain during a season of emphasis on giving. Giving is something that comes into their lives and brings joy. There is a change that happens in their hearts; they love to give because they know the blessing of giving.
>
> The Bible says in 2 Corinthians 8:12: "For if the willingness is there, the gift is acceptable according to what one has, not according to what he does not have."
>
> The Bible is teaching equal sacrifice, not equal gifts. Not everybody can give the same amount, but everybody can make a sacrifice. Show people how they can give more. People give when you make it possible for them to give. How do you do that? Well, two ways. Show them how to decrease their expenses and show them how to increase their income.[31]

Sample Frequently Asked Questions and Answers

When do I give to the campaign?

Giving to the campaign is a marathon, not a sprint. Giving of this magnitude will take three years for many people to complete. The giving period begins in March 2021 and runs for three years, through March 2024. Some people will choose to give weekly, monthly, quarterly, yearly, randomly, or in one lump sum. All of these options work for us. Many will set up recurring e-giving via the website.

How do I give to the campaign?

Over the three years, we anticipate that people will contribute through all of the ways that people currently give to our church. This includes credit and debit cards, EFT, ACH, online banking bill pay, checks, cash, non-cash assets, transfers of stock, vehicle donations, and more. And all of the ways we receive contributions are still in play as well: e-giving through our website, in the offering pouch/basket, in the mail, etc. The staff is available to help answer any questions about giving that you might have. Give us a call or send us an email anytime.

What if I cannot give right now?

We totally understand that not everyone has the financial margin to give "over-and-above" or "extra" funds. We have always been a place rooted in grace and freedom. Grace says there is nothing we can do to earn or lose God's favor because He has already shown us His love in the gospel. That is how we feel about people in the church family whether they give or not. And, we have always upheld the freedom to say "not at this time" or "no thank you" to any of the opportunities to give.

Should I reduce my regular giving to support the campaign?

Please do not. Our church has a ministry-focused general fund budget that depends on the faithful tithes and offerings of our congregation. Capital campaign giving is "over-and-above" giving and over a three-year period.

How will financial progress be reported to the congregation?

We've created this custom website for the purpose of updating you on the progress of each exciting project. This site is packed with images and videos that tell the story of what God is doing through our church. Come to the updates page for up-to-date information on our construction, global efforts, and all the exciting moving parts of the campaign. We'll be sure to keep you updated via email and social media too. If you haven't followed our social channels yet, the time is now!

Questions to Consider

How do we define vision at our church?

Who is responsible for the church's vision articulation? Where is it stated—signs, website, bulletin, etc.?

What percentage of our congregation could explain that vision?

What percentage of our congregation has embraced that vision as their own?

Have we come to a clear consensus on what the capital project is? If not, who is responsible for achieving that clarity?

Could we use a tune-up around our discipleship of people in generosity? Why or why not?

Who in addition to pastoral staff could be a catalyst for teaching principles of sacrificial giving and openhanded living?

Chapter Twelve

Three Platforms for Communication

Not surprisingly, communication and media can be the busiest feature of creating a capital campaign. This can become particularly stressful as the extra communication needed is being crafted while the church is conducting day-to-day business that does not go on hold so it can prepare for the campaign.

The Aly Sterling Philanthropy group offers a lot of help on their website, including an approach to communications strategy that is designed for non-profits. Think about how to reshape some of the actions below to apply to your church setting:

Communications During the Design Phase

1. Plan out your capital campaign and set specific fundraising and communications goals.
2. Prepare your capital campaign website, brand and slogan, and case for support.

3. Identify your target audience and message, and brainstorm strategies for how to interact with donors.
4. Hold in-person meetings with your largest donors to solicit major gifts.

Communications During the Public Phase

1. Kick off the public phase with an event where you announce your capital campaign to your wider audience.
2. Use a variety of channels—social media, email newsletters, flyers, etc.—to spread the word about your capital campaign.
3. Create a schedule for when you'll send out your communications.
4. Incorporate your capital campaign's branding on all your materials.[32]

The church may not use words like *brand*, *donor*, *solicit*, etc., but it is helpful and affirming that much of what we have covered in this book is similar to what experts in other philanthropic fields adhere to. Of course, not everything from the wider philanthropic community needs to be borrowed by the church, but we can learn from their expertise.

I find it easiest to categorize the conversation regarding media into three areas or platforms into which everything falls. We will list examples under each area with explanations. This is a baseline approach to communication strategy:

Print

Video

Digital

Print

Printed media is still a significant part of our culture. Ironically as brick and mortar bookstores close by the thousands, people still buy physical books (though they may order them online). And people still like to hold paperwork in organizational settings. Church campaigns are no exception—something still needs to be handed out or mailed out in addition to everything we may choose to do digitally.

Brochures

Whether this is designed and collected into one main print piece or divided into multiple handouts, there is certain content that needs to get into people's hands:

1. *Vision-Driven Project Explanation:* This "main" piece answers the questions "What are we doing?" "Why are we doing it?" "And how will it make a difference?" If only one print piece is done, this is it; and if paired down to a singular print piece, content from the next two sections would also be included.

2. *FAQ and Project Specifics:* The Frequently Asked Questions (or Q & A) document can be very helpful in addressing the common questions associated with any capital campaign. It can also address specific questions about the church's campaign focus. When there is construction or renovation involved, this second wave can also contain renderings and floor plans to provide a visual explanation.

3. *Giving Journey and Instructions:* This content is the guidance that people need to engage the campaign "ask" both seriously and spiritually. These are the spiritual principles to review that allow everyone to think, process, discuss, and pray about their eventual financial commitment to the campaign. It also includes the tactics on how and when people will respond in terms of the pledge process.

Invitations to Events

Often churches will create special meetings to engage with members of the congregation to expand on what they hear in worship services. With advanced planning, invitations branded for the campaign can be printed.

1. *Large Events:* Some churches will have dinners or programmed events with hundreds of people either at the church or at an off-site venue. This can be on one or multiple nights (which would require more than one set of invitations).

2. *Medium Events:* Another version of a gathering involves less people and can be either an affinity or ministry group (men's ministry, women's ministry, deacons, session, consistory, Sunday school class, etc.) or a gathering of financial contributors that is around forty to fifty people. This is often multiple nights or times and will require separate sets of invitations for each event.

3. *Small Events:* Churches that design home gatherings or small group gatherings (fewer than twenty people) will need invitations for this type of engagement.

There are some tactical decisions that need to be made about whether a church will print the contents of these invitations in advance, as often the details of multiple small events will be different—location, date, time, host, etc. This is the most nuanced print communication.

Spiritual Engagement and Curriculum

It can be easy to lose spiritual sight during the public phase of a campaign. To prevent this, churches may choose to provide opportunities to grow the faith of the congregation along with their generosity. This can take on a wide variety of characteristics to reflect the diversity of theology, style, and methodology of each church.

Here are some examples:

1. *Devotional or Prayer Book:* Churches may choose to custom design and write the copy (narrative, questions, Scriptures) for people to read once per day during the public phase of the campaign.

2. *Small Group or Sunday School Curriculum:* If a church has a built-in system of groups and classes, it may choose to use this delivery method to insert teaching and discussion about the project or bible-based generosity or both.

3. *Church-Wide Study:* With advanced planning from the teaching pastor or pastors, the church can coordinate an individual study book to correlate with the teaching during worship services. In this case, everyone would receive a study guide that they can use either individually, as a family, or in their group or class.

Branded Print Matter

There are choices to be made about how to make a consistent communication strategy once a title and brand for the campaign has been chosen or designed. The following are some building blocks of a communications effort to consider.

1. *Commitment/Pledge Card:* Though there often will be an option to commit or pledge digitally, the pledges are often received in the context of a worship service on a specific weekend or Sunday. Churches may choose to print or make available envelopes for privacy when the congregation turns in their card.

2. *Letterhead/Envelopes:* For any correspondence that relates to the campaign, churches may choose to make their branding consistent by having a separate letterhead and envelope. Churches continue to move toward digital communication but there are still reasons to send out paper correspondence through the mail.

3. *Campaign Giving Envelopes:* Again, many churches are moving away from envelopes or don't use them solely for receiving gifts as digital platforms continue to increase in popularity and practice.

But if envelopes are still in play, a redesign is necessary on the current envelope system or an additional envelope designed and branded for campaign-related giving.

Video

When I first began coaching churches on capital campaigns in the early 2000s, a campaign video was still very optional and often only done by large churches. However, as communication and media have radically changed over the last twenty years, a campaign video is imperative. It is the most common way to communicate in our culture—especially something that is important or emotive in nature. Video is now virtually nonnegotiable for a church capital campaign.

I recently met with DJ Hurula, Principal and Creative Director at ONE Brand Studio. I appreciated the way he talked about video, since it is what he does on a regular basis for churches and faith-based organizations. Here are some of the thoughts he shared with me:

> So much of a capital campaign's success depends on the ability to paint a vivid picture of the envisioned future. A campaign's media and creative assets must answer two pivotal questions: What does success look like? And, if we achieve the goal, how will our community be different? Print and traditional media have a role to play. They shouldn't be neglected. But video is the most important tool for communication. That's because video is the most emotive medium. Ultimately, people make decisions to give primarily based on feeling, not intellect.

Of course, it goes without saying that appealing to emotion at the expense of intellect is not what we are aiming for, nor should we be emotionally manipulative. Nonetheless, God has made us emotional beings, and we should not neglect appealing to emotions for fear of being manipulative. We should appeal to whole persons—intellect *and* emotion.

What does this look like practically?

1. *Main Video:* Because a video is a consistent media form that can communicate information as well as emotion and spirit, it is highly recommended that some form of a vision-based campaign video is created and shown. Much of the flow and storyboard can be based off the content of the main print piece. It almost always contains a clear financial "ask" from the senior pastor or a visible leader of the church and generally runs eight to ten minutes in length for use in the larger worship service setting.

Here are frequent content sections or scenes in a church campaign video:

- Connect the capital investment with the church's vision
- Inspire people by painting a picture of what God could do
- Include personal stories and testimonials
- Describe some specifics without overloading with detail
- Show video animation or architect fly-through of the project
- Mirror the information in the main brochure
- Explain the financial details and call to commit

2. *Main Video with Different Content:* The main video will often be shown more than once because of multiple worship services and events. Taking the main video and adding to it (or subtracting

from it) creates a second option for smaller meetings. A talented editor can efficiently make two or more versions or "cuts" of the main video.

3. *Supplemental Video:* With a specific project emphasis (renovations, children, outreach, missions, etc.), there can be a need for a video that highlights more details or specifics than the main video can contain without being too long. This supplemental video can be used in meetings as well as posted on the website, and it is usually shorter in length than the main video being used in worship services.

The Story Arc of a Church Campaign Video

Where we've been: This is a brief history of the church, testimonies of how God has used the church over the years, what has led the church to the point of starting this campaign. It might include quotes from various members of the church's role in their life. This might also include a timeline or historical photos of the church over the years.

Where we're going: This section casts the vision for the campaign. What are the goals and objectives of the campaign? What will the church and its ministries be able to do as a result of this effort? This includes appropriate photos of buildings/artist renderings, etc.

How we'll get there: This is the call to action for the campaign. A challenge to your people to participate in the campaign through their gifts, prayers, time, etc. This might include giving charts, key dates, prayer requests, etc., to engage your people in the campaign.

Digital

1. *Campaign Landing Page:* A typical approach to capital campaign communication is to create a dedicated landing page or section of the church's website where people can access all campaign-related materials.

2. *Digital Versions of Print Matter:* Because brochures and booklets are digitally designed, it is easy to make them available and downloadable from the church website.

3. *Digital Options for Giving and Pledging:* Most churches that already have a digital giving option can make an adjustment to allow for a way to pledge to the campaign digitally. It is especially helpful if the church's database management system has a pledge-tracking field that can automatically receive that digital pledge.

4. *Campaign Video(s):* Any videos created for the campaign can be available online as well as any sermons or messages delivered during the public phase.

5. *Social Media:* If a church staff regularly uses social media platforms to communicate with the congregation, then a social media strategy should be employed for the campaign.

6. *Mass Email:* An effective email strategy can allow for members of the church to stay aware of campaign events, sign up or RSVP, and link to campaign information and videos.

Virtually everything can be digitized or uploaded so the basic rule of communications is that anything created for the campaign should be available on the church website.

Starting a Media Items Inventory

When putting together the print, digital, and web communication for a campaign, churches can start with this simple yet non-exclusive lineup of items:

1. Main Campaign Brochure (printed and digital)
2. Main Campaign Video (shown in worship, meetings, and on website)
3. Optional Additional Brochure/s (FAQs, Renderings, Giving Guide)
4. Optional Additional Video/s (testimonials, more detail about projects)
5. Pledge Cards & Envelopes
6. Website (on church website or separate URL)
7. Invitations & Envelopes (to events, gatherings, etc.)
8. Campaign Letterhead & Envelopes
9. Banners, Posters, Renderings, Signs, etc.
10. Small Group Curriculum
11. Church Devotionals and Prayer Guides

Extras for Excitement

The following items are negotiable or "extra" for an effective campaign. Some churches have a culture of giving away "swag" during major events or happenings in the congregation, so items like these would be great options.

Other Options			
1.	Magnets	Mugs	Stickers
2.	Posters	Signs	Banners
3.	Shirts	Hats	Bracelets
4.	Kiosk	Display	Building Design Drawings

Figure 12.1

Primary Communications Considerations

1. *Outsource or In-House:* One of the first questions to answer is whether or not the church has the bandwidth, personnel, and time to take on campaign communications. There is the option to outsource to a trusted partner of the church or utilize a strategic partner of one of the reputable campaign consulting firms.

2. *Communications Calendar:* With the help of the navigator or consultant, a communications calendar can outline the dates for the completion and delivery of each communication piece as well as the distribution methods and dates.

3. *Quantities of Each Piece:* With the communications calendar in place, the amount of each print piece can be determined. If printed pieces are inserted, handed out, and/or mailed out, a determination can be made on quantity.

Brochure Printing Example	
Brochures distributed in worship, mailed to every home, extras available...	
Worship Attendance	500
Database Total Homes	800
Extra for Distribution	200
TOTAL PRINT OF EACH BROCHURE	**1500**

Figure 12.2

Questions to Consider

What has been traditionally strong about our communication and media systems? Give them a grade (A–F, like in school):

Print Grade: __________
What could be improved?

Video Grade: __________
What could be improved?

Digital Grade: __________
What could be improved?

What, if anything, should be outsourced for the campaign initiative?

List the strategic partners or professionals we would prefer to use:

____

____

____

Is there a way we could harness the campaign needs to help us improve communication going forward?

Chapter Thirteen

Three Features of a Campaign Gathering

Usually in a church capital campaign effort, worship services become the main gathering to communicate with the congregation. Additionally, there is merit to creating gatherings outside the context of worship services specifically for the purpose of talking about the campaign.

As mentioned earlier, the rule of thumb for engaging with people about their gift is, "the larger the gift, the smaller the meeting." In other words, if the pastor wants to discuss the lead gift or a major contribution to the church, this is often done in a private one-on-one or pastor-with-married-couple setting. The pastor (or appropriate key leader) may take them to lunch or dinner, etc. This is discussed in detail in chapter 10.

A more general discussion about prayerfully considering an over-and-above gift can and should happen during worship services where hundreds or even thousands may hear the challenge.

To begin strategizing, consider the Large-Medium-Small framework:

1. What will we do with people in worship regarding the campaign since this is our largest attendance at any gathering?
2. What is our approach if we were to run an event—like a dinner or gathering at the church or an offsite venue?
3. If the size of the discussion were more like a small group or home group, what would be the strategy?

These can be as creative and contextual as the church wants to make them. For example, a Lutheran church in the Midwest has a pattern of bringing people out for trivia competition and socializing, so they utilized one of those trivia nights to talk about the features of the campaign.

Some churches will plan an event in a restaurant or country club. Some congregations would perceive such events as too lavish, so an old-fashioned potluck, barbecue, or picnic would be a better choice.

The gatherings can be based on groups and classes, geography, age and stage, or other factors. Often, we suggest the church consider segmenting the giving population. As discussed in chapter 10, there should be a different approach to someone who is a consistent and faithful giver versus a less developed member of the congregation. Everyone is at a different place in his or her journey toward generosity.

For a meeting regarding capital projects to be effective, the content of the meeting needs to include three key elements:

Vision

Lay Person Testimonial

Challenge

Vision

At this point in the campaign, the vision for the church has been honed and creatively captured. There are materials available—print and video—that can be used to enhance the vision casting moment. Most have heard "people give to vision" as a way to remind us all that we cannot simply describe the features of a project without inspiring people with the potential results of a successful campaign.

One tool to help you shape the communication of vision is the spider diagram (figure 13.1) from the book *Church Unique* and used by the Auxano team. We regularly train communicators to utilize the "six ingredients" represented by the tool to make the moment of articulating the vision—whether it takes five minutes or fifty—as compelling as possible.

One fantastic way to gain the competence of crafting an inspirational message is to listen to great speeches from history and analyze how these messages are made and why they are so successful. Even a quick study of Martin Luther King Jr.'s "I Have a Dream" speech or President Kennedy's "Man on the Moon" address will reveal how the six ingredients work beautifully to motivate and inspire.

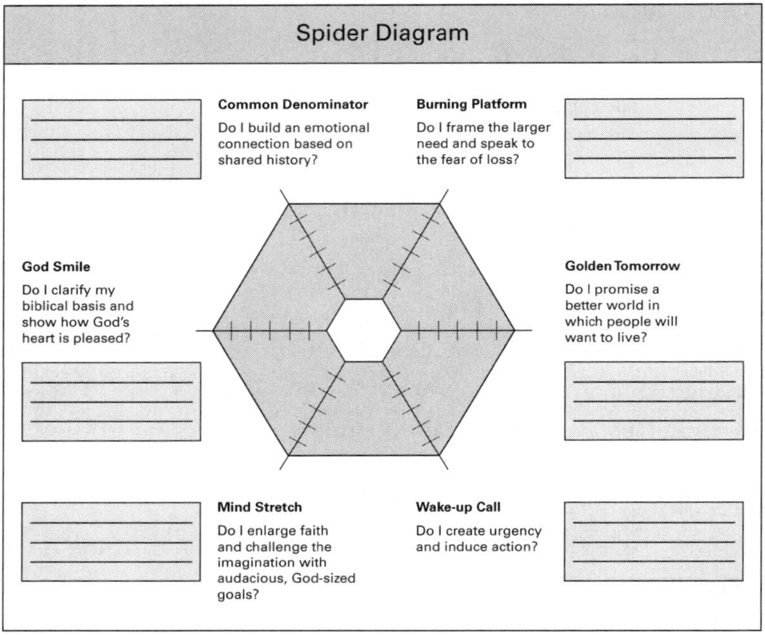

Figure 13.1

Lay Person Testimonial

An effective component of a campaign is when we hear a testimonial or story from a person other than the pastor. First of all, it is helpful when the congregation is driving both the future and the funding of that future. Having a compelling testimony from a lay person helps avoid the perception that the campaign is the pastor's "pet project" and hindering the success of the campaign. When it is a campaign by and for the congregation because of a clear understanding of the need, it eliminates any hint of the pastor's undue influence.

Rick Warren illuminates, "I hate to admit this as a preacher, and I hate to admit this for all of us who are preachers; but in many ways, a testimony about giving is 1,000 times more effective than a sermon about giving because people see a model. They see someone who has done it. They see someone who has taken the challenge and caught the vision. The Scripture becomes alive because people see what is happening in someone's life."[33]

Telling a Five-Minute Giving Story

Over the years, I have coached people to craft a personal testimonial by, first of all, calling it a "Five-Minute Giving Story." Calling it this tends to calm nerves and set expectations before we get into the nitty-gritty of coaching someone about what to say.

In summary: It's short. It's about giving. It's a story.

Sometimes words like *testimonial*, *stewardship*, *sermon*, or *challenge* can be intimidating to someone preparing to share their story. The following are the things a "storyteller" will want to know.

Elements of this story

- Brief—five minutes (no more than ten)
- Personal—not a sermon or speech, but conversational in tone
- Specific—a glimpse of how the person makes spiritual decisions about giving illustrated with personal examples
- Challenging—contains a "please join me" element where a soft challenge is issued for others to give as well

"Will it sound like bragging if I talk about my giving?"

If the highlights of your story include the recognition that everything we have comes from God (including our next breath), it is very difficult to make this a brag session. It is a deeply humbling thing to be aware of and articulate the provision of God in one's life and to say "the least I can do is invest into God's work, since it is God's money anyway." It is almost always a great spiritual exercise for the storyteller and a heart-warming and challenging moment for the hearer.

"I thought we weren't supposed to talk about our giving."

Yes and no. Certainly the Bible indicates that parading your spiritual acts in a way "to be seen" by others and admired is not appropriate. At the same time, Scripture also indicates times when spiritual leaders talked about their giving as an act of modeling generosity (think of David in 1 Chronicles 29). Imagine if no one had ever told you about giving and its importance in the Christian life? We need models for everything—to show and explain how to pray, be compassionate, worship, and give. Of course, this doesn't mean you need to give exact dollar amounts, but it can certainly be helpful and motivating to the community to share with some level of specificity.

Some Advice on Developing Your Story

- Practice by saying it out loud once or twice.
- Write it down to organize your thoughts and build your confidence.
- Don't make a speech—say something from the heart.
- Talk about who modeled generosity for you.
- Be specific about how you decided what you will be giving.
- Use the why, how, how much format.
- Invite people to join you in the process.

What do people want to know as they are evaluating their giving?

- Is it a worthy cause?
- What are others doing?
- What do you expect from me?

Questions to ponder and pray about:

- Why? (What is motivating me to join in the over-and-above giving?)
- How? (What way will I make a sacrifice to be able to give more?)
- How much? (Can I figure out a way to indicate a gift level to show the seriousness with which I am taking this opportunity?)

Pray and think about *why* you are considering an increase in giving, *how* you plan to rearrange your life, priorities or finances to be able to accomplish this, and then roughly *how much* that amount will be.

Sample 5-minute Giving Story Format

Hello, my name is ___________. My family and I have been coming to this church for ten years and have been so blessed by the teaching, fellowship, and opportunities to serve. We originally came here because ___________.

I don't know what our family would be like if we didn't have this extended faith family. I remember the time ___________.

We are really excited about this campaign and the projects that we are funding. I am especially excited about ___________. We are willing to go above our regular giving to support this for the next few years. We have had some time to think and pray about this so we just wanted to share briefly with you.

We knew we wanted to take this seriously, so the way we decided what to give was ____. That means we can give at least ____ over the next few years. We are excited and humbled to do this. Our family has been blessed with this resource and we know it all comes from God. We couldn't think of a better way to invest this than in our church at this moment in time.

One of the reasons we are sharing this is to practice the discipline of being thankful to God. Also, it holds us accountable to never think that we have anything other than what God allows. Finally, we want to ask you to join us.

Would you consider making a gift to the church that represents a sacrifice for you? We will, of course, never know what you choose to do, but we want to ask you to consider this with great seriousness and prayer. Thank you!

Challenge

This is a giving campaign. We need to ask people to give. As Henri Nouwen notes:

> Asking people for money is giving them the opportunity to put their resources at the disposal of the Kingdom and to offer people the chance to invest what they have in the work of God. Whether they have much or little is not as important as the possibility of making their money available to God.[34]

Each gathering or event needs to make the financial request part of the campaign clear. The temptation may be to have a feel-good experience that celebrates the church and soft-peddle or down-play the fact that a capital campaign is happening.

I call the challenge an "over-and-over" statement or request. Indicating that the gift is *over* the regular giving will help stabilize the operating budget during the time of capital investment. It is also *over* a certain period of time.

It is best when the ask contains a repeatable over-and-over phrase like "Please prayerfully consider a commitment to give over and above your regular giving to support the projects of the Forward to the Future campaign over the next two years."

People need to know what is being asked of them. It is ideal if we add to this challenge statement the date by which we are expecting people to respond. Something like, "And please be ready to join all of us in making that pledge on November 11" will be necessary.

Planning Events and Meetings

This is one of the opportunities for a lot of involvement and fun. These meetings will be thoughtful and meaningful, but don't need to be staid or stuffy. The church can really have fun with these. There are more details about meetings and the teams who may be responsible to design and execute these meetings in chapter 5.

1. Churches have utilized settings like:
   - Homes
   - Church Fellowship Halls
   - Restaurants
   - Hotel Banquet Rooms
2. The meetings frequently contain elements like:
   - Desserts & Beverages
   - Campaign Leader Vision Cast
   - Campaign Videos
   - Lay Person Testimonial
   - Media Handouts
   - Senior Pastor Short Message
   - The Ask

Questions to Consider

What are the reasons why some meetings should be smaller than others when it comes to discussing the campaign?

What type of gatherings have worked for us in the past and in what way can we be creative during the campaign? What seems like the best venue for the people of our church to connect?

A very basic agenda for a gathering is:

- Welcome
- Video Shown
- Vision for Campaign—Campaign Leader
- Questions and Answers
- Lay Testimonial
- Challenge—Pastor
- Closing Prayer

How could we modify this to create excitement and customize it to our style?

1. ______________________________

2. ______________________________

3. ______________________________

4. ______________________________

5. ______________________________

6. ______________________________

Who are the best event planners that we could tap to help lead and plan in a creative way?

Who in addition to the senior pastor is an effective and compelling communicator and could cast vision to our congregation at these events?

Chapter Fourteen

Three Questions in the Giving Journey

At some point, when the questions are starting to slow down about the projects, and we are still weeks away from Commitment Sunday, people will still need some guidance. This is when your guidance will focus on their prayers and deliberations about what they may choose to pledge to the campaign.

There are a number of ways we can coach people to arrive at "the number," but one of the simple ways is through the Giving Exercise. It is a spiritual exercise that entails asking oneself three questions:

> **What could I *reasonably* give?**
>
> **What could I *reprioritize* and be able to give?**
>
> **What could I *rely* on God for in an exercise of faith?**

What could I reasonably give?

This is basically a financial question. Most people have a sense of whether or not they can or will give beyond their current pattern. Likely, they have an almost immediate sense of this. This question is more about logic and reason.

Though we may not ask it this way, it is almost like asking, "What could I give without praying about it much or even thinking about it too hard?" Many people may just stop right here. What we hope for in a faith-led and discipleship-driven capital campaign is that people will go beyond this and go on a journey to a new level of devotion and trust.

What could I reprioritize and be able to give?

This is a question of behavior and adjusting patterns. It is about intentional choices and changes and so much more. One on hand, this is a math question. Like calculating, "If I went out to a restaurant one less time per week, what could I give to the church?" It is beginning to stretch the spiritual muscles of giving up something for the sake of something greater or more meaningful. This can be a fun exercise for the individuals in the congregation.

When is the last time they took an audit of spending behavior and evaluated it in light of the meaningful work of God in the world? Especially for people in the first world, we have a level of discretionary income and resources that is unlike many other places.

David Putman, one of Auxano's Lead Navigators, has a clever way to invite people to begin brainstorming and praying about what could happen to their gift and their faith in this journey.

Reprioritizing Resources			
POTENTIAL RESOURCES	WEEKLY	YEARLY	3YEARS
Eliminate 1 meal out per week	$35	$1,280	$5,460
Eliminate 1 Starbucks per week	$4	$208	$624
Eliminate 1 rented movie	$6	$312	$936
Reduce entertainment/shopping		$500	$1,500
Reduce Christmas budget		$250	$750
Reduce vacation budget		$300	$900
Garage sale income		$200	$600
Everyone's spare change each day	$5	$260	$780
Increase cash giving	$50	$2,600	$7,200
Total 3 Years			**$17,750**

Figure 14.1

What could I rely on God for in an exercise of faith?

If the first question was about reason, and the second question about behavior, then this question is more directly about faith. This is the idea that anything we have been given comes from God anyway, so why not trust that He will backfill your giving with blessing in many different ways?

Over the collection period of a campaign, various things can happen that are unexpected. What about an unexpected bonus, tax return, inheritance, or commission? What if we trusted in a bit of the unknown and "put God's name on that resource" ahead of knowing that it is on its way? It is His anyway, so we can practice believing that God will supply abundantly, particularly for His purposes through our church.

There are different ways you can help facilitate this kind of thinking. One church actually made a calculator for givers during the decision-making process. You can provide a range of resources like a "live" calculator on the church website or a simple reminder card that gets distributed as part of the media.

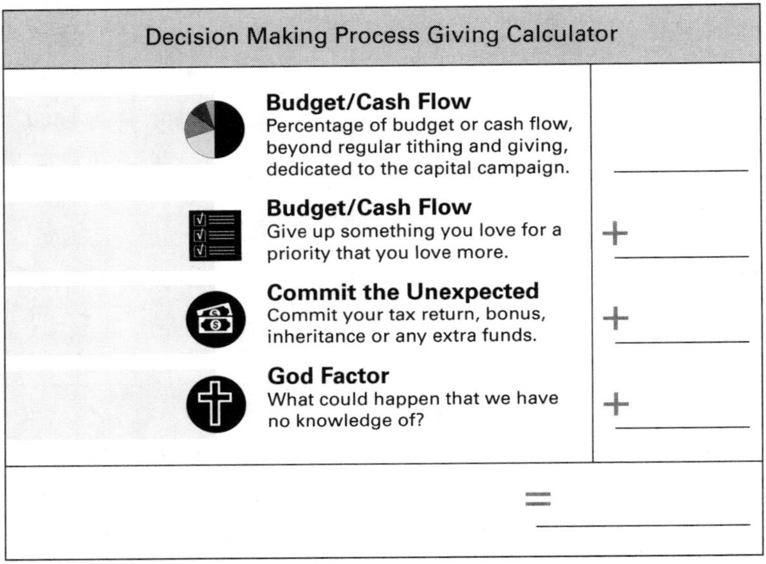

Figure 14.2

Questions to Consider

Is this something that would be well received at our church? Would we go so far as to distribute a guide to reprioritizing like the previous graphic?

Does our theology allow for the reasonable-reprioritize-rely motif of this advice for givers? If not, how else can we teach about our understanding of generosity and in what venues?

Chapter Fifteen

Three Unspoken Questions from Givers

Giving to the church can produce some anxiety for people. Sometimes it can create tension for couples that already struggle to talk about money. For others, guilt kicks in about not being able to give a large gift. The point is that there are a lot of internal battles that church leaders may never hear about as each household makes a decision about their response to a giving campaign.

By studying the psychology of giving and givers, we learned long ago that people are often asking a few things that they rarely verbalize. The following three questions have been in my head since my days at Cargill Associates. Dr. Robert Cargill was a pioneer in the church and university campaign world. He and his team developed many resources and techniques that I still use today. What we know from research and study is that these three questions are rattling around in most people during a campaign:

Is this a worthy cause?

What are others doing?

What are you expecting from me?

Alex Calder, Director of Development for Kensington Church in the suburbs of Detroit, has run two $20–25M capital campaigns as well as helped other churches around the country with similar efforts. He has interacted with thousands of people when it comes to their questions and concerns about "over-and-above" giving. His advice to churches trying to raise additional resources is to remember a few things in particular:

1. People want to know that you have done your homework.
2. People want to know that the goal is attainable.
3. People want to know that their gift counts.

Answering these unspoken questions and concerns can happen during the course of the campaign. That's why campaigns need six to eight weeks in design phase and six to eight weeks in public phase. People need time to hear things, ask things, and pray things.

You will need to answer these questions whether people ever choose to voice them or not. This is what goes into the communication and media (see chapter 12 on handouts, videos, etc.) and the modeling of targets, gift charts, and guides (see chapter 8 "Giving Constructs").

Is this a worthy cause?

We need to remember that the projects we are trying to fund with a capital campaign are not normal—they are "extra" in the minds of many. So, people aren't necessarily asking, "Is my church worthy of additional funding?" but are asking, "Do these special projects seem important enough for our church for me to get behind this and to what degree?"

Kyle Nabors, former Executive Director of Mercy Ships, describes his way of handling the question of worthiness in his leading others through a process of evaluation. He says that whether people realize it or not, they have an intuitive sense as to whether something is Critical, Important, or Nice to Have.

In other words, if we are not demonstrating the critical nature of a project, it will be much harder to garner financial support for that project. If something is perceived as nice-to-have but not necessary, then people will have a hard time investing in it.

What are others doing?

I have been surprised at the effectiveness of matching gifts. I am not personally motivated to give because of a match, so that has colored my view of this technique. I am not necessarily recommending this to churches (but have used it in a few instances where it was the best approach for a unique set of circumstances). But the reason I mention it is because of the unspoken question people tend to have, which is about whether or not others are participating:

Will I be the only one jumping in the deep end?

One of the ways I coach campaign leadership teams and church staff members during a campaign is to remember that we cannot be silent about our willingness to participate in a capital campaign. It is a personal decision to give, but it cannot be a secret.

Why do we not talk about giving as an important behavior and privilege of a Jesus follower? We mentor people in how to pray, how to read Scripture, how to minister to someone who is sick, visit someone in jail, teach a class, and more. But, we do very little to talk to our children, youth, and spiritual beginners (no matter what age they are) about the generosity that is a natural outgrowth of following a God who gave His Son for us.

Campaigns can be a time for the spiritually developed to model and even talk about how they learned to give, and why giving is an important expression of their faith. In an effort to help facilitate this need for modeling in the discipleship process, I developed a devotional exercise for people to begin to understand how to tell their story as a model for others to learn about giving from their personal experience. The devotional prompts people to sit down with a pen and "journal" their answers on their way to understanding their own giving story, often for the first time:

I first learned to give . . .

____

____

____

What I have learned over time about giving is . . .

____

____

____

I am committed to give consistently to my church because . . .

____

____

____

I normally give . . .

____

____

____

What are you expecting from me?

Most people want to do the right thing when it comes to their church, and most people in our churches have a pretty solid level of trust in the leadership, or they would go to a different church. Therefore, people need to be led in the area of giving. It is not natural for most to live with open hands, and being vague in our teaching is not helpful. Best practice campaigns offer discipleship and direction to people. You can still raise money without a discipleship-based campaign (people do it all the time), but that is not the mission of the church.

In a discipleship-based campaign, we can teach people:

- how to make spiritual decisions about anything (including money)
- how to listen for God's leading
- how to have a conversation with a spouse about money
- how to come to a decision about what to commit or pledge
- how to trust leaders even when you don't have every detail of a plan
- how to offer criticism without being angry or hurtful
- how to have a conversation with another person about giving

Seriously and Spiritually

I encourage church leaders to communicate to their congregation that the goal is for each of the individuals and families in the church to take the campaign both seriously and spiritually. To take it seriously means you give it time, attention, and focus. Attend the meetings, ask questions, read the materials, and engage with the ideas your church is considering for the future of ministry.

To take something spiritually means to engage in a spiritual process. It involves prayer, faith, devotion, discernment, and a sense of communion with the church body. If I am being spiritual about something, I am rehearsing what I know of the way God operates in the world and through people, then making myself vulnerable to the possibility that God could direct me in some powerful way.

The Giving Expectation

In 2 Corinthians 8:3, the apostle Paul commended a church for giving above and beyond. He wrote, "They gave more than they could afford, even beyond their ability" (author's paraphrase). How do you do that? Rick Warren teaches that people will either give by *reason* or they will give by *revelation*:

> Here is the difference between the two: When you give by reason, you have looked at what you possess, you have figured out what is in the bank. You figure out what is reasonable, and on the basis of that rational assessment, you commit that amount. It takes no great step of faith to give by reason.
>
> Now, the Bible says, "Without faith, it is impossible to please God." The Bible says, "Whatsoever is not of faith is sin." The Bible thinks using faith is an important factor, and we must teach faith in our churches. That is why God wants us to give.

He doesn't want our money. He doesn't need our money. He wants what it represents, our love and our faith and our trust and our surrender. So I can give by reason: I look at what I have, I figure out a reasonable amount, and I give that amount based on my current situation. But that is not the best example of giving by faith.

On the other hand, I can give by revelation. Revelation means that I determine my gift by praying, "Lord, what do You want me to give?" This is the question Kay and I asked when we made our commitment to our building campaign. That approach did not produce reasonable gifts. It produced a gift that God defined: "This is what I want you to give." He put it on my heart and on my wife's heart. When you make giving a matter of prayer, then your decision becomes an act of worship, not an act of reason. Does that make sense? We should teach our people not to give by reason but by revelation.[35]

Questions to Consider

What about our campaign projects and dreams would we categorize as Critical, Important, or Nice to Have?

List the project and circle your opinion of its rating among the three options:

Project 1 ________________

Critical | Important | Nice to Have

Project 2 ________________

Critical | Important | Nice to Have

Project 3 ________________

Critical | Important | Nice to Have

Project 4 ________________

Critical | Important | Nice to Have

Are there specific ways we can encourage people to consider their Giving Story?

In what way can we demonstrate that others have "gone before us" in their willingness to give? How can we not be silent?

Will leaders or staff pledge early? Can we announce that? Will it motivate people at our church?

Chapter Sixteen

Three Components of the Pledging Process

Since the campaign is ultimately a process that leads to a financial pledge, the pathway toward Pledge or Commitment Day needs to be clearly articulated. Whether people express these questions or not, they need pastoral and spiritual guidance about how to participate in the giving component of the campaign.

Some people have never experienced a church-wide giving campaign, and those who have, perhaps, have not done so in many years. Giving them specific guidance and stepping-stones along the way will put them more at ease so that a truly spiritual journey can occur. I believe many of the topics discussed in this chapter need to be addressed as soon as possible in the campaign, preferably in the design phase.

In chapter 11, I highlighted the kind of content that needs to be communicated and taught to enable the individual or family to regard the giving decision as a spiritual one. If a person or family is in this campaign process for about two months, having this information in a reference guide (brochure, web page, etc.) will be very helpful to supplement their prayers and conversations.

Three areas where the most questions occur are in the following categories:

Choosing an Amount
Pledge Process
Alternatives to Cash Giving

Choosing an Amount

Back in the day, my friends at Cargill Associates taught me a simple process for coaching individuals through the journey of deciding on an amount. See below this simple discernment process that any church can modify to fit their language, culture, and theology.

The key is that it is simple and do-able. Coach people to:

1. Pick an amount
2. Pray about that amount
3. Listen for God's leading
4. Leave room for faith

It starts with picking a somewhat arbitrary amount—this is based on the idea that most people have a sense for what they may be able to reasonably give from a financial perspective. Some would even say that each of us has a "default" gift size in our brains. We need to speak it out and begin the spiritual journey from there.

The second step is to pray a specific prayer that says, "God, I am thinking I should give $______ extra over the next few years to the church. Am I on the right track? Is this what You want from me?"

The third step is the listening ear. This is the exercise of discerning God's voice, and this listening process is unique for everyone. Sources for this "hearing" are God's Word, God's Spirit, God's people, and anything else in our world that may give us a nudge of spiritual guidance.

The fourth step is to leave room for faith. In the spiritual world, we need to allow for the possibility that God will lead in some way that will defy the odds or the norm. Christian history is replete with people who have lived this way. From Martin Luther to Martin Luther King, there are heroic and celebrated forms of going against the flow. But there are everyday heroes of the faith that act in a countercultural way all the time with their financial choices.

> Every time a family can't "keep up with the Joneses" because they made a sacrificial financial contribution to the cause of Christ instead, they are acting in this beautifully defiant way.

There is a special place of dependence, trust, and faith in God that lies between a careless approach and an overly conservative approach. On the one hand, a person can make a ridiculous and irrational pledge that may skew the church's campaign results in a detrimental way (say, if I were to pledge $10M because I know that God is capable of letting me hit the lottery). On the other hand, one could take such a conservative approach that they don't have to pray dependently or be in any wonder about how God may provide as they stretch their faith muscles. Both extremes take the faith factor out of the journey. Somewhere between these extremes is the excitement of an excellent church capital campaign.

Pledge Process

Some may bristle at the word *pledge*. I have heard this over the years more than a handful of times. A church member has a personal conviction about this (often basing it on Scripture) or has a personal concern that a pledge is a legally binding commitment. Either way, they would rather "just give" without pledging.

According to law, a pledge may be a legal contract, but state laws differ as to how enforceable those promises actually are. Interestingly, in the nonprofit sector, organizations are required to reveal pledges as part of their asset base. A simple internet search will reveal the legal fuzziness around this issue.

For churches, it is both a spiritual act as well as a budgeting practicality. The pledge (some will change this to the word *commitment*) can be a beautiful process of "laying it on the altar," a commitment to God as an act of worship. In many ways, the campaign is the spiritual journey toward one very special act or covenant. The budgeting practicality is that church leadership needs to have some sense of whether or not the money will be available to the church for the projects being considered.

So, in a very practical way, the pledge or commitment indication is a tangible way to communicate one's support to the leaders of the church. It is less of an iron-clad contract than it is a way to help those leaders fulfill their obligation to steward well.

We have Bible precedent for a public discussion regarding giving toward a campaign. A frequently cited story is the time of the building of the Jewish temple under King David's leadership. In Scripture we read that he was not bashful about raising money, investing money in God's work, talking with specificity about his own contribution to the cause, and challenging the leaders around him to do the same:

> Then King David said to all the assembly, "My son Solomon—God has chosen him alone—is young and inexperienced. The task is great because the building will not be built for a human but for the Lord God. So to the best of my ability I've made provision for the house of my God: gold for the

gold articles, silver for the silver, bronze for the bronze, iron for the iron, and wood for the wood, as well as onyx, stones for mounting, antimony, stones of various colors, all kinds of precious stones, and a great quantity of marble. Moreover, because of my delight in the house of my God, I now give my personal treasures of gold and silver for the house of my God over and above all that I have provided for the holy house: 100 tons of gold (gold of Ophir) and 250 tons of refined silver for overlaying the walls of the buildings, the gold for the gold work and the silver for the silver, for all the work to be done by the craftsmen. Now who will volunteer to consecrate himself to the LORD today?"

Then the leaders of the households, the leaders of the tribes of Israel, the commanders of thousands and of hundreds, and the officials in charge of the king's work gave willingly. For the service of God's house they gave 185 tons of gold and 10,000 gold coins, 375 tons of silver, 675 tons of bronze, and 4,000 tons of iron. Whoever had precious stones gave them to the treasury of the LORD's house under the care of Jehiel the Gershonite. Then the people rejoiced because of their leaders' willingness to give, for they had given to the LORD wholeheartedly. King David also rejoiced greatly. (1 Chron. 29:1–9)

The Modern Version of This Ancient Text

It may be a stretch to make this ancient description of King David's leadership something that is prescriptive for our modern churches. At the same time, it reveals some fascinating principles that still seem to hold true in the modern world.

1. Leaders lead the way in every category.
2. Challenging a group of people to support a worthy cause can be an effective way to stretch their faith and generosity.
3. Speaking about specifics regarding personal financial investment can be inspiring to others.
4. Tying our investment of "over-and-above" resources to our spiritual health and commitment is not unprecedented in Scripture.

Though Randy Alcorn expresses some concerns about pledges and "faith promises," he does indicate that this method can prompt trust, discipline, and ingenuity to earn and save money in order to give it to God. He refers to the Macedonians who were mentioned in Scripture for giving "beyond their ability" as an exercise of risk-taking faith. He reminds us that "God honors prayer, dependence, and generosity."[36]

In many ways, the culmination of the campaign is the Pledge or Commitment Sunday (or weekend). After members of the congregation have prayed and considered what they may give beyond their regular giving to the church, they indicate that amount via a response to the church—often a pledge card. Though many churches will have a digital version of this as well, most still use a physical card to represent the spiritual decision of giving a special offering to God.

Here are simple examples of a Pledge or Commitment Card. Most churches will consider the use of both a physical card and a digital option to register a pledge.

Pledge/Commitment Card Example

I'm in with genCity!

I/We have enclosed ____________ as our initial offering to genCity.

I/We are committing ____________ over the 36 months of genCity.

I/We anticipate giving ______ weekly, ______ monthly, ______ quarterly, ______ annually to our genCity commitment.

Name ____________

Address ____________

City ____________ State ________ Zip ________

Phone ____________ Email ____________

I'm In! We are committed to genCity.

A financial commitment to Bandera Road Community Church is not a legally binding contract. We ask that you give us an estimate so we can plan for our future. God tells us in 2 Corinthians 9:7, *"Let each one do just as he has prepared in his heart, not grudgingly or under compulsion, for God loves a cheerful giver."* If your financial situation changes, you may increase or decrease your giving level.

For your convenience, the giving chart to the right has been included to estimate your total gift over the 36 month period.

COMMITMENT SCHEDULE

Donors	36 Month Total	Annual	Monthly
1	$250,000	$83,340	$6,945
2	$100,000	$33,336	$2,778
3	$50,000	$16,668	$1,389
15	$25,000	$8,340	$695
80	$10,000	$3,336	$278
200	$21,600	$1,800	$150
300	$32,400	$1,200	$100
600	$1,200	$400	$33

Figure 16.1

Alternatives to Cash Giving

I received a phone call one day from one of the top givers at the church at which I was serving. The caller said, "Greg, I'm not writing one more check to the church."

I stayed calm and asked, "I'm sorry—what happened—is everything okay with you and your family?" He laughed and assured me that everything was fine and then said, "I can't believe

I never thought of giving stock as the main way to contribute to our church—I can give so much more and it helps both the church and our family a great deal." He decided to make quarterly stock contributions from that day forward. He remained one of the largest givers in a very large church.

A recent IRS report revealed that most of an individual's assets are not the pool from which they draw for donations. Another way of saying it is that people draw from the "smaller bucket" of their financial means. The asset bucket is much larger—but most of the conversation in campaigns seems to revolve around the cash-on-hand bucket which is generally a much smaller one.

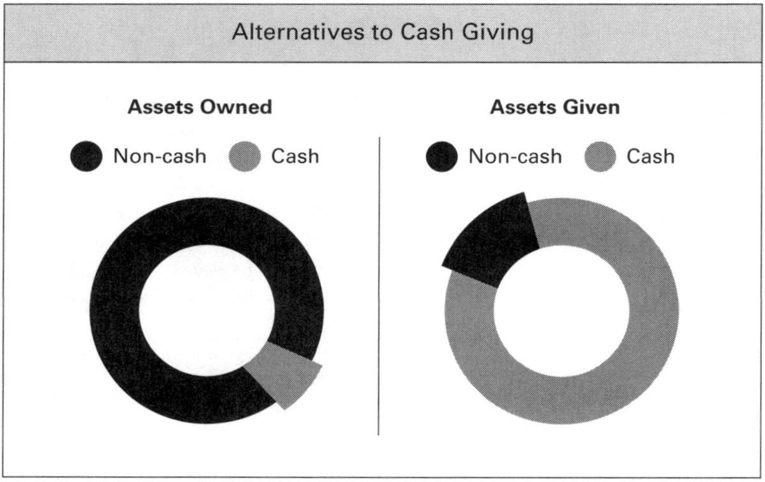

Figure 16.2

For many people in the church, giving non-cash resources is simply not something on their radar because the church has notoriously neglected these topics. I have heard story after story of a pastor finding out a church member made a sizeable contribution to an alma mater or a local charity (they usually find out because of a newspaper or internet news article). These other organizations are willing to ask for support, and they make very clear how the donor (your church member) could make significant gifts to their organization. They also do an excellent job of casting a compelling vision and connecting the impact of a gift to the fulfillment of that vision. (See chapter 8 on this topic.)

Please understand: I have no beef with the people of God being generous to organizations outside the church.

The problem is that so many church leaders have dreams and ideas and are frustrated, saying things like "I know our people could be much more generous." At the same time, they are not willing to have even the simplest conversations about the transfer of wealth to the church because it seems too indelicate, too secular, or they are simply scared that they will run off a church member. This conversation makes me think of a handful of things regarding the church and its reticence to talk about non-cash wealth transfer:

1. It reveals that other organizations have taken the science and psychology of giving and generosity way more seriously than most churches. They are intentional because they believe their cause is worth it.
2. It highlights the fact that churches are now in a somewhat competitive sphere—the arena of the challenge for charitable gifts. Years ago, pastors were not "competing" with such a massive sector of the economy that includes thousands of nonprofits vying for contributions.
3. It shows that when we emphasize cash flow giving or making sacrifices in personal budgets and spending, we are only asking our congregation to consider 10 percent of their wealth when it comes to the church capital

campaign. Especially for the best givers who are often giving 10 percent or more of their cash flow already to the general fund, we need to open up the conversation about the other bucket.

4. If you are reading this text in the first couple of decades of the twenty-first century, you have the potential to tap in to the largest wealth pool in history, which includes the transfer of wealth from the American Baby Boomer.

Whether you consider yourself in the evangelical camp or not, John Dickerson's work, *The Great Evangelical Recession*, has been eye-opening to many in the faith community. The team at Mortar Stone recently discussed the importance of understanding how to disciple generous givers and cited statistics from Dickerson and other places to highlight our anemic strategy to funnel wealth toward the church:

- Evangelical giving has decreased 20 to 30 percent annually since the fiscal cliff of 2009
- Donors who provide 68 percent of the current giving will no longer be living in twenty-four years
- People's wealth is 9 percent in their cash and 91 percent in assets
- 1.5M nonprofits seem to be battling for the 9 percent (only the cash part of wealth)
- We are in the middle of the largest wealth transfer in history—$41 trillion!
- This includes $4.6 trillion in business sales[37]

This is part of a much longer discussion addressed in my book *The Growing Generosity Playbook*; but suffice it to say that a capital campaign provides a platform to start informing people of these options to fuel the church. Very simply, your church can create a brochure (either print or digital) and explain the ways other than cash that are possible for giving to the capital campaign. Some would say that annual giving often comes from cash flow, but capital gifts may be derived from accumulated assets.

Here is a sample from a church I worked with years ago and comes from my friends at The Church of the Good Shepherd in Vienna, Virginia. This is just the narrative—it was designed, colored, and given campaign branding for distribution. Consider adapting this if it would be helpful for your church.

Ideas for Giving

This brochure makes general suggestions, but tax laws are complex, they change frequently, and your tax situation is unique. Please consult your tax advisor before making any decisions about non-cash gifts to the church.

Sharing out of our abundance

Normally, when we think of giving to The Church of the Good Shepherd, we think of giving out of our income. But wealth consists not just of what we earn, but also of what we have accumulated over time. As we consider prayerfully how we can best support Good Shepherd's Lighting the Flame capital campaign, we can reflect on other possible resources for giving as well. In some cases, usually for legal or tax reasons, these "nontraditional" gifts can benefit both Good Shepherd and the person or family making the gift—quite apart from the satisfaction you get from being generous and hastening the kingdom of God.

Here are some of the possibilities:

- Publicly traded securities
- Personal property
- Appreciated real estate
- Paid-up insurance policies
- Charitable lead trusts
- Gifts in kind
- Deferred gifts

Publicly traded securities

Giving appreciated stock or bonds is one of the most common ways to make capital gifts. With some limitations, you normally can deduct the full value of the securities as of the date of your gift—and neither you nor Good Shepherd will pay tax on the gain.

(For many members, having any stock that has appreciated over the last few years is something of a miracle. But some members may own appreciated stock because they can buy their employer's stock at below market prices, or because they got zero-basis stock as part of their compensation.)

For example, if you paid $2,000 for stock now worth $10,000, you could either:

1. Sell the stock, pay capital gains tax of up to $1,600, and keep $8,400;

   OR
2. Give the stock to Good Shepherd, get a $10,000 tax deduction, and lower your tax liability by $3,000 or more.

Personal property

You can give personal property (basically, anything that is not real estate) to Good Shepherd in support of the Lighting the Flame campaign. Items might include antiques, artwork, jewelry, coin or stamp collections, or even vehicles. Normally, these items are deductible at their fair market value; see your tax advisor for details.

Appreciated real estate

A gift of real estate will result in your being able to deduct the property's full appraised fair market value. As with securities, neither you nor Good Shepherd will pay tax on the gain. You might own a piece of real estate but want to realize some of the value for yourself. In that case, you might consider a "bargain sale."

For example, a member has a parcel of land that cost $30,000 but is now worth $50,000. She sells the land to Good Shepherd for $30,000 (her basis). She makes a deductible gift of $20,000 (the difference between the market price and the selling price) and also gets $30,000 in cash. (Good Shepherd would probably sell the land promptly and realize $20,000 in profit.) A win-win situation.

Paid-up insurance policies

You might have paid-up whole life insurance policies originally taken out to cover mortgage expenses or to pay for college tuition. If these reasons are no longer valid, a paid-up insurance policy can be an excellent way to make a gift to Good Shepherd.

You would get a deduction of the lower of the policy's replacement value or your cost in the policy. Good Shepherd would get the option of retaining the policy (deferring the gift until the insured person dies) or taking the current cash surrender value.

Charitable lead trusts

This one involves lawyers: You create a lead trust to provide income to Good Shepherd for a specific number of years. Then the assets in the trust revert back to you (or to people you name in the trust). Cash, securities, and some types of real estate can be used to fund charitable lead trusts. You would not get a current income tax deduction, but there is an estate tax savings.

Gifts in kind

A gift in kind is a tangible item that you can give, usually because of your work or related business, such as construction materials, landscaping, computers, lighting, flooring, office supplies, etc. Under current tax law, you can deduct the fair value of tangible gifts in kind. Unfortunately, you cannot deduct the value of services you render, such as legal advice, IT support, vocal performance, photography, etc. But it is possible to get the same effect by arranging to charge Good Shepherd for your services, then making a gift of cash back to Good Shepherd.

Deferred gifts

Deferred gifts are, simply, gifts whose benefit Good Shepherd does not realize until some time in the future. Until then, you retain an interest in and, usually, control over—the assets to be given.

Examples of deferred gifts include:

- Bequests
- Charitable remainder trusts
- Charitable gift annuities
- "Pay on Death" accounts
- IRA beneficiary designations
- Life insurance

Frankly, these can get somewhat complex. Good legal and accounting help are essential if you are considering a deferred gift.

Here is another sample from a church's capital campaign brochure that includes these alternate ways of giving:

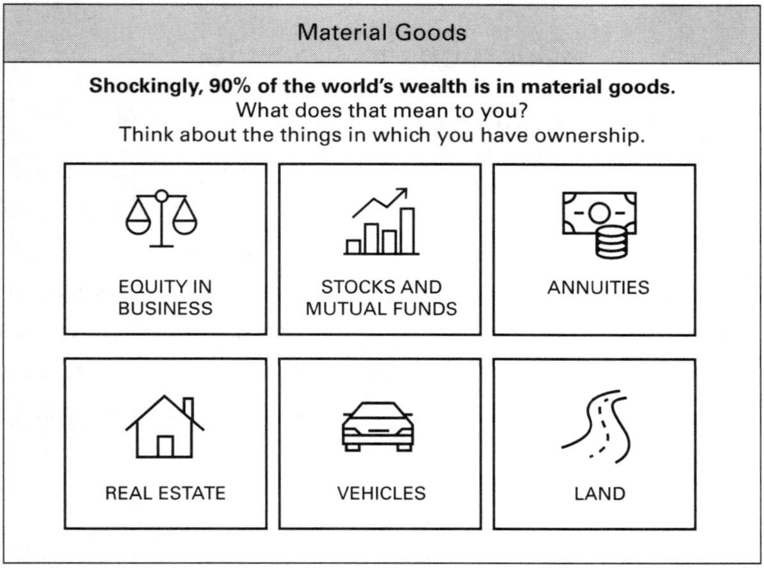
Material Goods
Shockingly, 90% of the world's wealth is in material goods.
What does that mean to you?
Think about the things in which you have ownership.
EQUITY IN BUSINESS
STOCKS AND MUTUAL FUNDS
ANNUITIES
REAL ESTATE
VEHICLES
LAND

Figure 16.3

Questions to Consider

In what manner can we teach people to regard the pledge or commitment in a serious way?

Do we have a way to receive a digital pledge?

How can we make the process of committing to the church campaign as much an act of worship and devotion to God as it is the register of a pledge?

Do we have the mechanisms in place to receive non-cash gifts?

Can we use the campaign to put in place the platform and information to encourage people giving from their 90 percent on a more regular basis?

Chapter Seventeen

Three Practices After Pledges

Most of the effort goes into engaging the congregation during the time of spiritual challenge surrounding the "ask" for financial support. The public phase of the campaign is the most visible and concentrated effort. Yet, the collection period is typically years following Pledge or Commitment Sunday. It is recommended that a plan of communication, celebrating, and reporting be developed for the collection period. This is often called the Follow-Up Strategy. Whether managed by staff or a Finance or Follow-Up Team, there are some basic considerations or questions to ask:

1. What are the communication mediums or platforms that already exist into which we could insert information, reporting, or celebration of campaign progress?
2. What should we add monthly, quarterly, or annually to make sure people are aware that

the collection period is important and faithful fulfillment of their pledge is a key to success?

In many ways, the follow-up phase requires just as much effort in a more gradual and methodical manner. It requires clear communication, updates, reporting, thanking, and more. Some churches will even see collections of more than 100 percent of what was originally pledged because they had such an effective way of encouraging people to give during this phase—they either collect more money than expected, more donating families than originally registered, or both. I highly recommend that during the planning and design phase, church leaders create at least an initial draft of their strategy for the collection years—a follow-up strategy.

That strategy should include at least these three practices:

Acknowledge and Thank
Celebrate and Communicate
Review and Renew

Acknowledge and Thank

It is a best practice of capital fund pledging that the churches acknowledge the commitment. There is both a relational component to this as well as a financial accuracy feature.

From a relational perspective, it is simply better to show gratitude and do it right away. This is often in the form of a letter from the senior pastor, but some churches choose to use the financial administrator to continue to keep the pastor pristine from knowledge of pledge amounts. A church could do both—a quick thank-you note from the pastor with no mention of the pledge amount, and acknowledgment of a specific pledge amount by the finance office.

In terms of accuracy, it is prudent to make sure the church has recorded the pledge or commitment correctly. This is simply showing that the finance office has a professional and accurate gathering of the information.

Either way, a letter can be sent that accomplishes this initial thank-you that has this tone:

> *Dear ____________,*
>
> *Thank you so much for participating in our Growing Forward campaign. It has been an exciting time.*
>
> *We have recorded your commitment over the next three years to be $5,000 and wanted to show our enormous gratitude. If for some reason we recorded this inaccurately, please let me know right away.*
>
> *Thank you so much—exciting times are ahead and you are a big part of that.*
>
> *Bill Smith*
>
> *Financial Secretary*
>
> *PS: When you receive your quarterly giving statements, the amount of your giving to Growing Forward will be included as well.*

Celebrate and Communicate

Adam Morris uses the prototype of the celebration from Nehemiah 12 as a way to encourage churches to celebrate God's provision, people's generosity, a God-honoring accomplishment, etc. When the wall was completed in Jerusalem, Scripture recounts that a party started. With multiple choirs, harps, lyres, cymbals, songs of thanksgiving, it was such a shindig that history indicates "the sound of rejoicing in Jerusalem could be heard far away." It reminds me of the half-time celebration at the Super Bowl, but with less immorality.

Okay, back to Morris:

What Should Anchor Our Celebration?

1. It should be worshipful. When believers give as an act of obedient worship, the ministry should worship God with them for His faithful provision.
2. It should be joyous. When reading Nehemiah 12, one can sense the pure joy at the party.
3. It must be God-centered. While God worked through certain members of the fundraising team to help channel the funds to the ministry, the team itself is not to be the center of attention. We are celebrating God's work in the hearts of believers.
4. It should reflect hearts of thanksgiving. Celebrations must acknowledge God's goodness and reflect a heart of thanksgiving for all He has provided.[38]

Creating Communication Systems and Patterns

A systematic approach to celebrating milestones along the way is the best approach. Typically, churches can start this conversation by brainstorming the way they will communicate campaign updates and collection progress. This is the modern-day version of the thermometer on the wall that fills in or fills up over time. What people need to know is, "How are we doing? Are people giving with the consistency that I am trying to show? Is the money coming in at the pace we expected? Has the pace of collection changed anything about our projects? Are we still starting them on time and finishing them when expected?"

One way to make an **initial draft plan** is to list the things that already exist in the church into which we could place campaign updates:

- Worship Service
- Church Website
- Church Newsletter
- Church-Wide Email Blast

Often Follow-Up Teams (lay people and/or staff) are assembled to deliver the information in winsome ways. A droning financial report from the pulpit like "We've collected X amount of dollars so far" is a bit bland without some forethought. One church in Florida gave out candy—"100 Grand Bars"—every time they collected another hundred thousand into the campaign account. This sweetened their communication.

More thoughts from DJ Hurula at One Brand Studio on how video can be used in this phase:

> Post-campaign communication is critical because it demonstrates accountability, shows respect to the donor and sets the stage for future asks. Don't handle "follow-ups" as an afterthought. Instead, schedule and budget for them as part of the overall campaign. At predetermined intervals, you must report back and show the outcomes that resulted from giving.
>
> Video is the most effective way to do this because it creates assets that can be used in many ways throughout the life of the church. A year after

> the campaign is complete, what are the stories that are emerging? How have lives been transformed by what was given—and even in the act of giving itself? What is happening now that simply could not have happened without the community responding as it did?[39]

Aside from video, there are a number of other ways to keep your givers updated on progress. Kensington Church, a large multi-site church in Michigan chooses to hold Celebration Dinners—opportunities to gather and thank givers over a simple meal, allowing leaders to cast vision and deliver updates about campaign projects and other ministry initiatives. At each dinner, slide shows or videos of the ways the money is being invested are a part of a short presentation.

Review and Renew

At periodic times during the collection period, the financial records should be reviewed to see if there are any trends that demand our attention. Some churches have a regular rhythm of analyzing patterns but not all churches do.

NOTE: A built-in tool for reviewing both personal and corporate giving toward the campaign is the quarterly giving statement. It is highly recommended that churches do a quarterly statement and then use that for vision-casting, updating, and encouraging faithfulness to the pledge.

Other tools for retaining attention:

Year-End Giving: When the church engages the congregation in November and December, it is a good time to make people aware of their progress-toward-pledge amount as individual households.

Pledge Renewals: At periodic times (often annually) churches can ask for a re-commitment from current givers as well as "cast a net" to see if new contributors might jump in.

Envelope System: For churches using envelopes, the distribution, branding, and use of envelopes can be tied to campaign giving and updates. For churches that don't have giving envelopes for each family, one-time envelopes can be used for a special giving opportunity at various seasons.

Email: Email provides the opportunity to communicate widely in an inexpensive way. It can contain information, encouragement, and links to campaign updates that may be on the church website.

Events: Update dinners or desserts with givers can be a winsome and easy-going way to gather people for information or encouragement to give.

Generosity Pathway: Developing a generosity pathway is a longer conversation but indicates the idea that a church has a systematic approach to discipling and nurturing givers whether a campaign is happening or not. It is a series of meetings, classes, and relationships that focus people on being generous disciples.

Alex Calder, development director at Kensington Church and national consultant on this topic, constantly reminds pastors that conversations about giving should not only be happening around capital campaigns or during the follow-up phase. This could be a great time to institute a new pattern of behavior. He advises "a significant part of the pastor's calendar and energy should be devoted to regular meetings with donors. Many of them desire spiritual counsel on these matters and are eager to listen and learn."

Needing a Little Nudge

There may be times along the way that an encouragement or challenge from the pastor could help with campaign funding. This is particularly helpful if there is a specific reason cited like, "If we can get up to $1M in our account, the builder can begin the project."

However, just telling people they are behind in their pledge fulfillment is not a motivator—and may not be fair since we coached them that God may provide for them anytime throughout the collection period. In other words, there are no parameters around when their gift is given—it could be all on the last day of the multi-year giving window.

Sometimes churches may choose to renew pledges and commitments. This often happens at the year-mark or the annual anniversary of the original pledge month. Some have even used a "Start Up, Step Up, Stay In" motif to allow for new pledges, increased pledges, and a renewal or recommitment of one's original pledge.

Start up, step up, stay in Commitment Card

Start up, step up, or stay in?

So far, 2,974 households have committed almost $22 million to seeing our mission fulfilled. In order to accomplish all the projects in this campaign, it takes significant financial resources from our entire church – the nearly 15,000 people who attend Kensignton regularly. As we approach the final year of this three-year campaign, we are asking everyone to prayerfully consider investing in the work of God through Kensington.

KENSINGTON
CHURCH

START UP
I/We commit to give $__________ per month for 12 months, now-March 2019 for $ __________ as a one-time gift).

STEP UP
I/We currently have a pledge of $__________ but we commit to increase our pledge amount to $__________ and will fulfill this new amount by March 2019.

STAY IN
I/We commit to fulfill our original pledge amount by March 2019.

Name(s): __________

Address: __________

____

Email: __________

Phone: __________

Campus: __________

kensingtonchurch.org/everyone

Figure 17.1

Start up, step up, stay in Commitment Card

CAMPAIGN

Every once in a while, an opportunity comes along that changes everything.

The Every[one] Capital Campaign launched in 2016 and requires significant financial investment to fulfill our mission to see every[one] transformed and mobilized by Jesus.

Every single detail in all of the projects has been carefully planned as we listen to God and discern His plan for us as we live to fulfill our mission as a church.

GIVING

GOAL $ 30M

Pledges (to date) $ 22M

PARTICIPATION *by household*

GOAL 5,000

Current 2,974

KENSINGTON *by the numbers*

Our average weekly attendance is: 14,241

# of giving households: 7,619

(of those, 2,974 give to the Every[one] Campaign)

START UP

This is for those that have not joined in on the excitement of the Every[one] Campaign yet—*please read*.

Jumping in now will make a huge difference! It takes every individual and couple that attends Kensington joining together to do their part to hit our goal. If you are new to Kensington or haven't made a pledge yet, it is time to live dangerously and ask: "God, how would you have me invest in your Kingdom through the work of Kensington?"

We're asking every individual and couple to pick a sacrificial gift amount so that we can hit our goal. To help us finish strong, you can choose a one-time gift or monthly giving for the next 12 months. We would achieve our goal if:

- 750 households commit to $50/month for 12 months (or $600 one-time).
- 1,300 households commit to $100/month for 12 months (or $1,200 one-time).
- 2,000 households commit to $250/month for 12 months (or $3,000 one-time).

(Consider the typical amount we spend per month at a restaurant, on coffee, on manicures, or on our golf game—simply choosing to not eat out once or twice a month could translate into an amazing gift over 12 months!)

STEP UP

This is for those that have completed their pledge (or are close). Has God blessed your financial situation over the last 2 years? Awesome—*please read*.

Like many people, you may be in a better financial position today than when you made your original pledge back in March 2016. Has your situation changed? Would you consider hopping on board at a new level for the last 12 months to make these projects a reality?

Hundreds of households have already completed their pledge (or are very close). We still have the opportunity to give over these last 12 months of the campaign, and we are so close to our goal—will you go beyond your current pledge to give a boost toward the finish line?

STAY IN

This is for everyone who made a 3-year pledge back in March 2016 and plans to fulfill it by March 2019—*please read*.

Thousands crossed the stage in 2016 and placed their commitment card in the box as an act of worship. These people made a faith pledge—an amount that could only be fulfilled with God's help. This campaign is only successful because you continue to give faithfully and consistently.

You made a commitment back in March 2016, and you're "staying in," letting us know that you plan to come across the finish line by completing your original pledge by March 2019. We need to know that, too! We are encouraging everyone that made a pledge to faithfully fulfill their commitment, so we can plan and budget accordingly.

Let's join together as a church by investing in the Kingdom of God to reach the [ONE] with the message of Jesus.

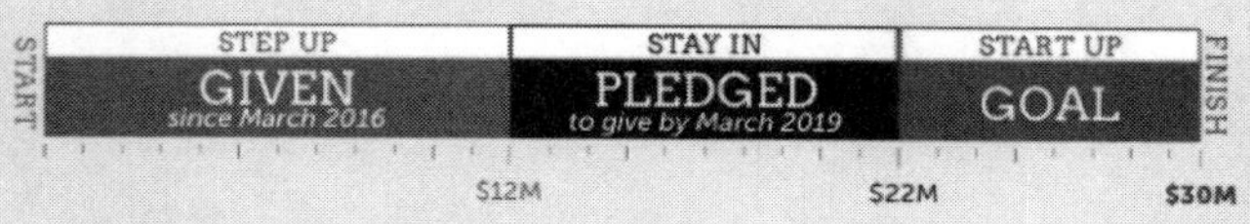

Figure 17.2

One way to organize the follow-up strategy is to look at what action or medium will be used monthly, quarterly, and annually. The follow-up or finance team can then execute the plan, making adjustments when necessary.

Follow Up Strategy		
Monthly Ideas	Quarterly Ideas	Annual Ideas

Figure 17.3

Questions to Consider

Who is responsible for follow-up and follow-through?

What can we practice in campaign follow-up that should become a regular part of our discipleship in generosity?

1. ______________________________

2. ______________________________

3. ______________________________

4. ______________________________

Do you agree or disagree with Calder's recommendation that "a significant part of the pastor's calendar should be devoted to regular meetings with donors"? Explain your view.

How can we celebrate giving in all of its forms? Is there a way to affirm and measure the behavior we are hoping to increase?

Appendix A

Raising Capital in Multi-Site Settings

Campaigns are special times in the life and history of any church. A well-run and successful campaign can give the spiritual and financial surge that enables churches to do some amazing things.

For those leading in a multi-site setting, there are a few challenges that a single location church may not face. Often, church leaders have some level of experience with raising capital. But we are now on a learning curve—understanding the differences of leading and raising money in a one-church-many-locations environment.

Every effective capital campaign will contain some basic components. Among those are:

- a clear and compelling vision
- enough time to cultivate a spiritual response
- leaders who lead by example
- an opportunity to educate about biblical generosity

But campaigns that carry a multi-site vision will need to go beyond juggling mailings, media, and great sermons about financial sacrifice. The following ideas are important to consider:

Cast a Vision Everyone Can Connect With

The main goal of a capital campaign is to raise money for projects that are beyond the regular flow of giving—it is a special surge of money for projects that cannot be funded by the general operating budget. But there are benefits beyond finding extra money when you bring everyone together around a common vision. The campaign causes everyone to ask some serious and spiritual questions like, "Is this church doing a kind of work that I can give my life to? Are they headed in a direction that I can invest in financially?" Campaigns are a time of challenge—they inherently test the commitment of the congregation because of the nature of the ask. And, it provides an opportunity to lift people's eyes up to the larger vision of your church movement. It will often afford members the opportunity to give in a completely beautiful and open-handed way as they fund projects that will never directly benefit themselves. In this unique setting of multiple congregations, the focus or vision of the campaign needs to keep in mind the wide variety of people who will hear and receive the challenge.

Understand How Each Campus Will Hear the Ask

Leaders think about the future all the time. And they think about the movement overall. It is difficult, however, to remember what it is like to be the one asked—hard to think and feel like a church member or attender. First of all, those who come to your church are experiencing it—the worship, the friendships, and the spiritual development. They are not thinking strategically about the implications and challenges of leading a large multi-site movement. They will see and hear through their own experience. The job of campaign leaders is to understand this to the best of their ability. Ask yourself, "How will the people of this particular location hear this? Is it easy for them to buy in? Does it impact their world? Are there parts of the campaign that will discourage them from supporting it financially?" Second, there is often a kind of sub-culture at each location or site. There is diversity, even if it is subtle, because it is all one big church with different meeting places. And as much as leaders would love to hear that people at each location are thinking about their site-siblings, they tend to think about the site they attend, not the ones they do not. So, the difference between this and a one location capital campaign is that there can be competing interests. This isn't bad—it is just the reality, and it needs to be understood in the decisions about how we communicate.

Anticipate Questions

One of the keys to leading well through a campaign is to anticipate the questions and criticisms people may have. It is very honoring to the congregation to have done the homework that shows you care about their hesitations. To say things essentially like, "you may be wondering how we arrived at this" or "we anticipate you may have some questions and we want to help answer them." In the early stages of roll-out, when people are hearing the ideas and projects for the first time, an FAQ page should be written already—before people even ask those questions.

Leave Enough Lead Time for People to Kick the Tires

Large congregations that are spread out geographically need even more time to hear and respond. The larger the movement, the more time is needed. Often, by the time a local campus leader verifies a response to a question with the "central office," it takes a few weeks just to make sure everyone is provided with proper information. Many churches are tempted to spend most of their time and resources on the public campaign. This is where most church leaders shine—creating public services and delivering ideas and information with high excellence and great inspiration. But don't overlook the importance of getting out the campaign information months and months before the actual challenge happens—and not just on Sunday mornings (or whenever you hold services). People in the church need time to ask questions, talk about it in the hallways, and chit-chat about it in their homes. They will give leadership the feedback and critique that is needed to know how to shape the campaign when it is time to go public.

Gain Wide Ownership from the Inside Out

The law of the concentric circles of communication is about informing people in a systematic way that breeds ownership. It is a way of communicating that starts with the leaders at the very inside of the organization and then moves to larger and larger circles of people until it reaches the least connected members of the church community—the ones on the fringe. This applies to change management, vision casting, and definitely applies to a high-impact capital campaign at a multi-site church. Once the vision for the campaign is drafted, it can be tested and refined through the circles of communication. By the time the leadership goes public, there is already a very strong sense that the campaign being executed has been "owned" by leaders, staff, high influencers, and some key financial contributors. Some churches will conduct a formal study to ensure buy-in before launch. Either way, the diversity of a multi-site demands a strong sense of ownership before investing horsepower in a major campaign.

Appendix B

10 Most Asked Capital Campaign Questions by Church Leaders

1. How much money can we expect to raise?

For many years, capital campaign consulting companies would refer to a statistic that uses the church's annual income (general offerings only) as the baseline—over a three-year period, the church can expect to raise 2–3 times that annual income over and above that giving toward a capital project. With the rising complexity of charitable giving (including the many organizations outside the church focusing on church members), there are now more factors than a simple multiplier. A savvy approach includes an understanding of immediate context—the things that impact the potential.

Every campaign has unique features, driven by things like:

- The makeup of the congregation
- The tenure of the senior leadership

- The focus of the project (debt, real estate purchase, renovation, etc.)
- The amount of time since the last fundraising campaign
- The local or national economy
- The church's approach to teaching generosity

2. How long does it take?

An effective campaign involves the church's leadership, staff, and body. A few months of preparation are needed to train as many as possible and communicate clearly before ever going "public" to engage the entire congregation. Then, it requires six to eight weeks in the public phase. The ideal scenario allows for a four to five-month process in total.

3. Will our regular giving decrease?

The common fear is that members of the church will "rob Peter to pay Paul." There is a way, however, to conduct a campaign so that regular giving not only is steady but increases. The way is to teach about biblical generosity and remind people that these important but extra capital projects are over and above their regular support. Campaign leaders need to carefully remind people that cannibalizing the general fund because of the allure of a special project may have the unintended effect of staff or ministry reductions because funding has decreased.

4. Are there times of the year that are better than others to campaign?

With few exceptions, the best time to run a capital campaign in a church is between Labor Day and Thanksgiving or between New Year's Day and Easter. Though most churches should avoid summertime because of vacations and lower attendance, there are churches in North America where the climate or location drives attendance up in the summer. Another exception to the rule happens when Easter falls very early in the calendar and it would require rushing the campaign to finish before Easter.

5. Do we have to use an "outside" consultant or coach?

Technically, no. The process of securing over-and-above capital funding can be done without a consultant. There are basic principles that, if employed, will produce good results both in the spiritual life of the congregation as well as in the financial support. However, few churches (who may do this once every few years or even longer) can do this as effectively as a professional who does it every day.

The outsider provides:

- A well-traveled perspective, bringing both ideas and trouble-shooting tips collected over many campaigns
- Accountability to a time line, process, and tasks that can be customized but are proven to be effective
- A temporary "staff" member for the campaign, since the current pastors and staff are very busy with their assigned responsibilities
- A perspective that is not emotionally attached to any project or person, bringing a fresh approach

6. Do people actually give the money they pledge?

A fear can sometimes exist that people will be emotionally moved to pledge a certain amount but have no ability to fulfill that pledge. If the church largely bases or even begins a project on the pledge total, then unfulfilled pledges can be a huge challenge.

Disruptive events during the pledge period can certainly stall pledge returns—change in leadership, significant changes to the project, congregational or staff conflict, etc. As a general rule, however, people are faithful to their church. If leadership tends well to the process and communicates along the way, most churches will receive more than 90 percent of what was pledged. Unique factors may even drive this higher—sometimes over 100 percent.

7. Will people who don't normally give financially step up if the capital campaign is exciting?

Since campaigns tend to necessitate some effective teaching about biblical generosity, stewardship, intentional living, and other powerful principles, people tend to make great strides during this time. The special part of this is that people who are not regular givers may choose to start giving faithfully to the church's general offering while they are declining to give over and above. At the same time, it also becomes very clear that givers are givers and people who are looking for a reason to not give will find the reason no matter how effectively the campaign is executed.

8. Can we get funding from outside groups, grants, foundations, and corporations?

Because of the passion surrounding the project, churches often wonder if there are other groups that will supplement the giving done by the members of the church. This is motivated by a desire to succeed, and sometimes by a desire to not put the burden of a capital project entirely on the backs of the congregation. There are certainly occasions where this can happen, but those are few and far between. Many companies and foundations have restrictions in regard to religious institutions, and ones that are favorable toward the church rarely will invest in a capital project. It is certainly not bad to ask (one of the chief rules of fundraising), but enormous amounts of time invested by a church seeking "outside" money can often be better spent cultivating gifts from within.

9. How much should it cost to raise this money?

The costs associated with raising capital in the church are associated with the size and complexity of the campaign. Some churches choose to reimburse the general budget out of the campaign proceeds once they start to come in. Costs are not directly tied with the amount of money raised, nor do church consultants get a percentage or commission on the total.

The costs should be fairly predictable, can be budgeted for, and are a result of a few things:

- **Production:** costs related to media (video, print materials, signs, logos, etc.)
- **Distribution:** costs connected with any mailings, mass email, or social media
- **Hospitality:** food, décor, and other costs connected with meetings and events
- **Consultation:** most consultants are paid a negotiable flat fee for services

As a percentage of the total raised, costs tend to be between 4 and 6 percent. Because many of the costs are not tied to the amount raised, this cost-of-money-raised percentage will be higher for smaller campaigns and lower for large campaigns.

10. Can we raise money to pay down debt?

Yes. Churches can often see a surge in cash flow when money that was once used to service debt can now be deployed for programs, ministry, and staffing. The burden of the campaign leadership is to make the case that a) the debt was not incurred irresponsibly and b) there will be an actual ministry benefit to the pay-down of debt. This is a more challenging campaign to navigate but is done regularly by churches on the heels of a major building project or to advance a certain ministry idea that is being held up by funding.

Appendix C

Reasons to Consider Consultation

I placed this discussion in the appendix to the *Capital Campaign Playbook* for a few reasons. For one, it is not a tool or technique to use in the planning of a capital campaign like the chapters of the book represent. And another reason is that placing it early in the book would look like a direct strategy to drum up consulting work for our team and me.

Many may not even read this since they have already made their decision to either use or not use a strategic outsider. But, if you are still reading, this could help if you are still in the throes of deciding whether or not to invest in a coach.

Common reasons for outside help include:

1. Church has never done a campaign before (or hasn't in recent history).

2. The pastor and staff have "full plates" already—expecting them to add the responsibility of a self-led campaign seems to be an overreach.
3. Campaigns led by a professional outsider garner more funding—it actually could become a stewardship breech to not hire as opposed to a stewardship victory by saving money.
4. If the campaign doesn't produce the results that the church hoped and prayed for, the consultant takes the blame. We don't want the pastor to live for years under the cloud that "the campaign that Pastor Bob ran didn't work so well."

Having given and received consulting over the last few decades, I think there are three ideas to consider:

Process
Expertise
Perspective

Process

Many churches choose to bring in one of the reputable consultants or consulting firms because of process. This means that instead of reinventing the wheel, they simply ascribe to a process that is proven and provided by the outsider.

This book set out to make the point that there are a handful of things to do that have been developed over the years, and they are pretty much contained in the previous pages. But some will see that all of the ingredients sitting on the kitchen counter don't make a cake. The consultant is experienced at walking the church leadership through a series of steps (making customized adjustments along the way) to achieve the church's goal for capital funding.

Consulting firms charge thousands of dollars, but churches are often aiming to raise hundreds of thousands if not millions. The cost-benefit analysis seems to still be in favor of hiring someone from the outside. Penny pinching isn't always an ideal posture when it comes to a monumental chapter for the church—and you can't redo pledges or process if things don't turn out the way the church had hoped.

The benefits of consultant to the process can include:

1. Accountability to stay "on task"
2. Keeping pace so the campaign doesn't drag or delay
3. Ownership by the church's leaders because they have invested church resources
4. Trouble-shooting by an expert when needed

Expertise

Like in any other industry, there is a special skill set that comes along with traveling the country as a church consultant. You have seen variations, addressed unforeseen challenges, and learned how to navigate the idiosyncrasies of churches and their leaders.

In *Outliers*, author Malcom Gladwell contends that 10,000 hours of practice allows someone to be an expert in their field. He cites that these hours allowed the Beatles to become the greatest band in history (thanks to playing all-night shows in Hamburg) and Bill Gates to become incredibly successful and rich having used a computer more than most ever since he was a teen.

Again, church leaders can know all of the secrets of how to be an expert in a field (like the field of capital fundraising). But having not used those tools often means there is a level of risk to "trying" in a real-time and high consequence situation in your church.

Will Mancini shares his thoughts about campaign consultants on his blog:

> In 1999, when I served on the pastoral team of Clear Creek Community Church, we engaged a well-known campaign consultant. The experience was mediocre at best. It felt slick and tacked-on. I never sensed that he cared too much about our church. In the end we decided as a team that we wouldn't do it again. It was a beautiful opportunity to learn what not to do as a church consultant. When it comes to campaign consulting, I have found that I'm not alone. In fact, I have been having increased conversations recently with people in the industry and pastors who have had good and bad experiences. It seems there are four primary reasons that pastors aren't so crazy about calling someone to help with their capital campaigns:
>
> - The cost seems high for what you get.
> - What you get reflects common industry knowledge.
> - The campaign program isn't adaptable to the leadership culture.
> - The campaign program isn't genuinely spiritual.[40]

Will is a straight-shooter. But he is also a consultant, so he is aware that good ones are worth their weight in gold. But he may be articulating what you have felt or struggled with. Perhaps you can use this as a template:

1. Evaluate the cost-benefit and compare fee structures.
2. Find a consultant that shows expertise beyond "common industry knowledge."
3. Ask if there is an adaptive or custom nature to what they do.
4. Make sure the approach is spiritual and discipleship-based.

Perspective

Having a third party or outside perspective is critical in these intense times in the life of a congregation. Very simply, it is difficult for any organization to not be "too inside" to see what needs to be seen. And often for churches, there are high loyalties and emotional connectedness that can cloud judgment.

An outsider can also help reinforce what the senior leadership or senior pastor has been saying all along. Sometimes the leadership's words have lost their punch because of the "prophet without honor" principle. As strange as it may seem (and as frustrating as it can be for pastors to hear their words through someone else), the outsider saying the same things can pack a power that is used for the good of the church.

Appendix D

Budgeting for a Capital Campaign

Among the key decisions to running a capital campaign from an expense perspective is whether or not a strategic outsider (consultant) is used and to what degree. Some consultants have virtual options that are less expensive than "onsite" coaching.

Another decision is in regard to whether or not the "soft costs" related to building analysis, feasibility, and design (architect fees) are accommodated by the campaign proceeds.

The following grid presumes a full engagement by a reputable church capital campaign consultant.

Typical Expense Considerations

1. Communications and Media: design, print, video, web
2. Event Design: décor, food, room rental, sound equipment
3. Consulting Fees: capital campaign consultant

For many church campaigns, the "cost of raising funds" is plus or minus 6 percent of the total. This percentage is (of course) less with larger campaigns. And this is simply an approximation to help church leaders get a sense for what to expect.

A church that raises $500k will often pay up to $40,000 in expenses

Cost of Funds Raised: 7 to 8 percent or 8 cents for every dollar

A church that raises $1–2M will often pay up to $60,000 in expenses

Cost of Funds Raised: 4 to 6 percent or 6 cents for every dollar

A church that raises $2–4M will often pay up to $80,000 in expenses

Cost of Funds Raised: 3 to 4 percent or 4 cents for every dollar

Source of Funds for Campaign Expenses

1. Reserve funds
2. Budgeted funds
3. Future funds (pay back from campaign proceeds)
4. Combination of the above
5. Major donor family seed gift

What is the estimated cost for your church at this point, and what is the likely source of funds to cover that expense?

Appendix E

Campaign Readiness Checklist

DESIGN

1. Case for Support

Biggest Challenge:	Communicating with precision and clarity
Primary Concern:	Connecting projects with vision
Key Features:	Answers to the 5 Questions of Clarity

2. Calendar

Biggest Challenge:	Competition with existing patterns
Primary Concern:	Commitment or Pledge Sunday
Key Features:	Meetings, trainings, events, worship

3. Communications

Biggest Challenge:	Copy writing and content
Primary Concern:	In-house or outsourced leadership
Key Features:	Print, video, web

4. Branding

Biggest Challenge:	Eye-catching without going overboard
Primary Concern:	Choosing a title
Key Features:	Color and design palette

5. Target

Biggest Challenge:	Assessing and estimating correctly
Primary Concern:	To not stretch too far
Key Features:	A goal or tiered goals

6. Pastor

Biggest Challenge:	Calendar impact
Primary Concern:	Energy and health
Key Features:	Messages and meetings

DISCIPLESHIP

7. Teams

Biggest Challenge:	Recruiting busy people
Primary Concern:	Staff vs volunteers
Key Benefit:	Ownership and help

8. Training

Biggest Challenge:	Right amount, timing, and pace
Primary Concern:	Job descriptions and objectives
Key Benefit:	Creates energy and advocacy

9. Discipleship

Biggest Challenge:	Engaging people on spiritual journey
Primary Concern:	Use of curriculum (or not)
Key Benefit:	Spiritual growth and progress

10. Segmentation

Biggest Challenge:	Strategy for each segment

Primary Concern:	How to engage the top 20%
Key Benefit:	Effective use of energy

11. Events

Biggest Challenge:	RSVP process
Primary Concern:	How many at what size?
Key Benefit:	Information and inspiration

12. Follow-Up

Biggest Challenge:	Perseverance
Primary Concern:	An effective strategy
Key Benefit:	Pledge retention

Notes

1. https://churchexecutive.com/archives/five-reasons-why-churches-limit-the-length-of-capital-campaigns

2. Ibid.

3. Shared with the author in a personal conversation with Dr. Clint Grider.

4. Chuck Klein, "Why Shorter May Be Better for Your Church," Impact Stewardship.

5. http://famousquotefrom.com/billy-graham/

6. Shared with the author in a personal conversation with David Putnam.

7. Stephen Covey, *The Speed of Trust: The One Thing That Changes Everything* (New York: Simon & Schuster, 2006), 1.

8. https://www.causevox.com/blog/build-trust-with-donors/

9. https://www.willmancini.com/blog/short-circuited-dreams-3-ways-your-last-capital-campaign-actually-hurt-your-church

10. https://www.kotterinc.com/8-steps-process-for-leading-change/

11. http://www.ronniefloyd.com/blog/5855/pastors/when-you-are-casting-vision/

12. http://www.cru.org/content/dam/cru/legacy/2012/03/Catching-and-Casting-a-Vision.pdf"

13. http://en.wikipedia.org/wiki/Pareto_principle

14. Sean Mitchell at https://generositydevelopment.com/2015/11/30/a-capital-campaign-of-prayer-2/

15. Randy Alcorn, *Money, Possessions, and Eternity* (Carol Stream, IL: Tyndale House Publishers, 2003), xii.

16. Personal sermon notes on "Teaching Your People to Be Generous" by Rick Warren and Tom Holladay.

17. David Kinnaman, *The Generosity Gap* (Ventura, CA: Barna Group, 2017), 63.

18. http://www.barna.com/research/christians-financial-motivations-matter/

19. Steve Andrews, *Life with a Capital "L"* (Rochester Hills, MI: Harpist Miner Publishing, 2020).

20. Henri J. Nouwen, *The Spirituality of Fundraising* (Nashville, TN: Upper Room Books, 2011), 4.

21. In some cultures and contexts, wealth is not as much of a factor in getting things done as it is in America. At the same time, we see evidence in the early church that there were men and women who funded what the early church was doing.

22. Ben Witherington III, *Paul's Letter to the Philippians: A Socio-Rhetorical Commentary* (Grand Rapids, MI; Cambridge, U.K.: William B. Eerdmans Company, 2011), 8.

23. Kim Klein, Klein & Roth Consulting, "Getting Started in Fundraising," www.slideshare.net/careleaf/kim-klein, slide 18 of 46, Kim Klein,

24. Email from Clint Grider to author.

25. https://www.pastormentor.com/major-donors/

26. Ron Haas, *Ask for a Fish: Bold, Faith-Based Fundraising* (self-published, 2013), 43.

27. Simon Sinek, *Start with Why: How Great Leaders Inspire Everyone to Take Action* (New York: Penguin Group, 2009), 228.

28. James Belasco and Ralph Stayer, *Flight of the Buffalo: Soaring to Excellence, Learning to Let Employees Lead* (New York: Warner Books, Inc., 1993), 90.

29. Nouwen, *The Spirituality of Fundraising*, 3–4.

30. Todd McMichen, "Growing Beyond Church Debt," https://www.religiousproductnews.com/articles/2008-August/Feature-Articles/Growing-Beyond-Church-Debt.htm.

31. Sermon notes from Rick Warren and Tom Holladay, "Teaching People to Be Generous."

32. https://alysterling.com/capital-campaigns/

33. Sermon notes from Rick Warren and Tom Holladay's "Teaching Your People to Be Generous."

34. Nouwen, *The Spirituality of Fundraising*, 25.

35. Sermon Notes "Teaching Your People to Be Generous," Rick Warren and Tom Holladay.

36. Alcorn, *Money, Possessions, and Eternity*, 247.

37. https://mortarstone.com/next-generation-philanthropy-asset-based-giving-strategies/

38. Adam J. Morris, "Organizing Fundraising to Transform Stewards to Be Rich Toward God" in *Revolution in Generosity*, ed. Wesley K. Willmer (Chicago, IL: Moody Publishers, 2008), 260.

39. Email correspondence from DJ Hurula and the author.

40. https://www.willmancini.com/blog/4-things-pastors-want-in-a-capital-campaign-consultant